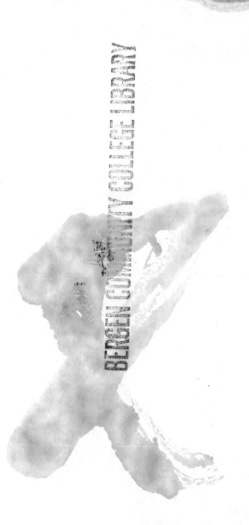

LORCA AND JIMENEZ: SELECTED POEMS

LORCA
AND
JIMÉNEZ

SELECTED
POEMS

Chosen and Translated by
ROBERT BLY

BEACON PRESS

Boston

Beacon Press books are published under the auspices
of the Unitarian Universalist Association

Published simultaneously in hardcover and paperback editions

Simultaneous publication in Canada by Saunders of Toronto, Ltd.

9 8 7 6 5 4 3 2 1

Library of Congress Cataloging in Publication Data

Bly, Robert, comp.

  Lorca and Jiménez: selected poems.

  Text in English and Spanish.

  1. Spanish poetry—20th century. 2. Spanish poetry—Translations into English. 3. English poetry—Translations from Spanish.

I. García Lorca, Federico, 1898–1936. Selected works. 1973.

II. Jiménez, Juan Ramón, 1881–1958. Selected works. 1973.

III. Title.

PQ6187.B5   861'.6'208   72–75536

ISBN 0–8070–6394–0

ISBN 0–8070–6395–9 (pbk.)

Selected Poems of
JUAN RAMÓN JIMÉNEZ

From DIARY OF A POET RECENTLY MARRIED

Selected Poems of
FEDERICO GARCIA LORCA

JUAN RAMON JIMENEZ
UNDER THE WATER

I

No matter which poems of Juan Ramón Jiménez I had chosen, the collection would never be a heavy book, like a book of Neruda or Trakl. A single poem of Trakl's would make a heavy book. Forty poems of Jiménez will be light as a feather. Juan Ramón Jiménez' vision of poetry is very different from that of Neruda or Trakl. Neruda and Trakl take all their weight as men, and put that into their poems. Their love goes out as a form of occult energy into boulders, river barges, crumbling walls, dining rooms, women's clothes. When they step back, they leave the energy there. Their poems lie there separate from them, massive, full of grief. To Jiménez writing a poem means something entirely different. For him a poem has ecstasy: that is the difference between poetry and prose. Living as a poet means feeling that ecstasy every day of your life, every hour if possible. A poem flies out of the poet like a spark. Whatever the poet writes down will be touched with ecstasy— the poem will therefore be light, not light in the sense of light verse that avoids seriousness, but light as a spark or as an angel is light. With one or two fewer words the poem would leap straight up into the sky.

The heavy poems of Trakl lie brooding in alleys or on mountain tops, and when the reader walks up to them they hardly notice him: they feel too great a sorrow. Jiménez' poems on the other hand are nervous and alert, and when we come near, they see us, they are more interested in us than in themselves—they try to show us the road back to the original ecstasy. The poems are signposts pointing the reader back to the poet, that is, back toward the life from which the ecstasy came. Juan Ramón Jiménez said that he lived his life in such a way as to get the most poetry possible out of it, and he loved solitude, private gardens, cloisters, silent women with large eyes.

Jiménez' poems ask the question: what sort of life shall we live so as to feel poetry, ecstasy? His emphasis on how the poet *lived,* rather than on rhythm or technique, is precisely why so much poetry flowed from him into the young poets. In his life he embodied as Yeats did some truth about poetry that everyone, but especially poetry professors, try to ignore and do ignore.

II

We can understand the subject matter of Jiménez' poems if we understand that it is in solitude a man's emotions become very clear to him. Jiménez does not write of politics or religious doctrines, of the mistakes of others, not of his own troubles or even his own opinions, but only of solitude, and the strange experiences and the strange joy that come to a man in solitude. His books usually consist of emotion after emotion called out with great force and delicacy, and it must be said that his short, precise poems make our tradition of the long egotistic ode look rather absurd. Seeing the beauty of a sunset, for instance, he does not, with many stanzas, complicated syntax, and involved thoughts, write a long elaborate ode on immortality—he simply says:

> Serene last evening,
> short as a life,
> end of all that was loved,
> I want to be eternal!

Translated by
Carlos Francisco de Zea

This is what he calls "naked poetry." It is poetry near the emotion. He has a wonderful poem in which he says that, in his youth, when poetry first came to him, she came to him like a very young girl, naked, and he loved her. Then, later, she began to put on ornaments and become very elaborate, and he began to hate her, without knowing why. Then, years later, she began to trust him, and now, at last is a young girl, naked, again—"naked poetry, that I have loved my whole life!"

III

Jiménez, as a poet, was born in the great and joyful reviving of Spanish poetry about 1905, led by Antonio Machado, Unamuno, and himself, who all dreamed of a new blossoming of Spain. Jiménez was not robust. He was delicate, neurasthenic, and slipped off into insanity more than once. Yet his devotion to poetry was healthy and rigorous. He was more generous to younger poets than Yeats was; he spent years editing poetry magazines and starting publishing ventures to get poets in print, endless afternoons poring over young poets' manuscripts. His delight and Machado's stubbornness prepared the way for the great generation of '28: Lorca, Aleixandre, Salinas, Guillén. They all knew it. Lorca's early poems are imitations of Juan Ramón, as they always called him. Juan Ramón threw up light and airy houses made out of willows, and in so many different designs that all the coming Spanish poets found themselves living in one or another of his willow houses before they moved out to their own house. Jiménez even anticipated Lorca's mature work. Juan Ramón Jiménez came to the United States in 1916 to marry Zenobia Camprubí, who was the sister of a man who owned a Spanish-language newspaper in New York. Jiménez lived in New York and Boston for a few months, and wrote

3

Diary of a Poet Recently Married, a book about the United States still not well known here. Thirteen years before Lorca he met the "King of Harlem" walking up Fifth Avenue; he describes the meeting in his prose poem "Deep Night," translated in this collection. The crippled Negro whom he calls "king of the city" is clearly the same Negro of whom Lorca said:

Tú, gran rey prisonero, con un traje de conserje!
(Your great imprisoned king, dressed as a janitor!)

Anyone who knows the work of Guillén, Salinas or Alberti will also see Juan Ramón Jiménez in their poems, seated quietly on the sandy bottom, clearly visible through the sunlit water, like a magic water creature.

IV

By 1940, most of the poets of that magnificent blossoming of poetry were either dead or in exile. With Rafael Alberti, Jorge Guillén, Pedro Salinas, Emilio Prados, Manuel Altolaguirre and Luis Cernuda, Jiménez went into exile. He lived for a while in Chevy Chase, Maryland, then in Puerto Rico. The American literary community ignored him, and not a book of his had ever been published in the United States at the time he received the Nobel Prize.

His love for his wife was one of the greatest devotions of his life and he wrote many of his poems for her. When he received the Nobel Prize in 1956, his wife was on her deathbed; he told reporters to go away, that he would not go to Stockholm, that his wife should have had the Nobel Prize, and that he was no longer interested. After his wife died, he did not write another poem and died a few months later, in the spring of 1958.

v

Jiménez and Rubén Darío, the Nicaraguan, gave a great gift to Spanish poetry: an emphasis on pleasure. Herbert Marcuse in his *Eros and Civilization* talks of how many Americans are crippled because of the puritanical adherence to duty, to the reality principle. They are crippled because they are addicted to boring sobriety, harshness, duty, "responsibilities of life," business. They think it is their duty to accept boredom in politics, to stay inside on a moonlit night, and to be miserable, selling or teaching, doing what they don't want to do. If they avoid delight, they feel more mature. Americans are crippled because they give up, perhaps at ten or fifteen, all hope of being happy. Juan Ramón Jiménez is aware of all this—only the Spanish temperament is as puritanical as the American. His work pulls the psyche toward pleasure. His poems are an elaborate defense of the pleasure principle. He sees the humor and drama of making such a defense today. He talks to the full moon:

> The basil is not asleep,
> the ant is busy.
> Are you going around naked
> in the house?

—ROBERT BLY

5

Roots and wings. But let the wing grow roots and the roots fly.

—JUAN RAMÓN JIMÉNEZ

from

Early Poems

Rimas de Sombra   (1902)

Arias Tristes   (1903)

Pastorales   (1905)

Poemas Májicos y Dolientes   (1909)

La Frente Pensativa   (1912)

El Corazón en la Mano   (1912)

Pureza   (1912)

Sonetos Espirituales   (1915)

ADOLESCENCIA

En el balcón, un instante
nos quedamos los dos solos.
Desde la dulce mañana
de aquel día, éramos novios.

—El paisaje soñoliento
dormía sus vagos tonos,
bajo el cielo gris y rosa
del crepúsculo de otoño—.

Le dije que iba a besarla;
bajó, serena, los ojos
y me ofreció sus mejillas,
como quien pierde un tesoro.

—Caían las hojas muertas,
en el jardín silencioso,
y en el aire erraba aún
un perfume de heliotropos—.

No se atrevía a mirarme;
le dije que éramos novios,
. . . y las lágrimas rodaron
de sus ojos melancólicos.

ADOLESCENCE

We were alone together
a moment on the balcony.
Since the lovely morning
of that day, we were sweethearts.

—The drowsy land around
was sleeping its vague colors,
under the gray and rosy
sunset of fall.

I told her I was going to kiss her;
she lowered her eyes calmly
and offered her cheeks to me
like someone losing a treasure.

—The dead leaves were falling
in the windless garden of the house,
and a perfume of heliotrope
was still floating in the air.

She did not dare to look at me;
I told her we would be married,
—and the tears rolled
from her mournful eyes.

"YO ESTABA JUNTO A MI MESA"

Yo estaba junto a mi mesa
y entre mis flores, leyendo
el libro triste y amargo
del poeta de mis sueños.

Ella se acercó callada
y me dijo: —Si los versos
te gustan más que mis labios,
ya nunca te daré un beso.

—¿Vienes conmigo? ¡La tarde
está tan hermosa! Quiero
antes que llegue la noche
ir por jazmines al huerto.

—Si quieres, vamos; y mientras
cojes jazmines, yo leo
el libro triste y amargo
del poeta de mis sueños.

Me miró triste; sus ojos
llenos de amor, me dijeron
que no. —¿No quieres? Voy sola . . .
Entonces seguí leyendo.

Con lento paso, la pobre
se fue, sufriendo en silencio;
se fue al huerto por jazmines . . .
y me quedé con mis versos.

"I WAS SITTING"

I was sitting near my table
among my flowers, reading
the bitter and melancholy book
of the poet who knows my dreams.

She came to me silently
and said: "If the poems
please you more than my lips,
I will never give you another kiss.

"Are you coming? The dusk
is so beautiful! Before
it gets dark I want to pick
jasmines in the garden."

"If you want to, we'll go, and while
you're picking jasmines, I'll read
the bitter and melancholy book
of the poet who knows my dreams."

She looked at me sadly; her eyes
with love in them said no
to me. "Don't you want to? I'll go alone . . ."
Then I went on reading.

She walked slowly, the poor
creature, suffering in silence;
went to the garden for jasmines . . .
I stayed there with my poems.

11

Iba vestida de blanco.
Despúes mis ojos la vieron
llorando y cojiendo flores
allá en la sombra del huerto.

She was dressed in white.
Later my eyes saw her
crying and picking flowers
there in the darkness of the garden.

"LAS CARRETAS"

Ya están ahí las carretas . . .
—Lo han dicho el pinar y el viento,
lo ha dicho la luna de oro,
lo han dicho el humo y el eco . . . —
Son las carretas que pasan
estas tardes, al sol puesto,
las carretas que se llevan
del monte los troncos muertos.
  ¡Cómo lloran las carretas,
camino de Pueblo Nuevo!
  Los bueyes vienen soñando,
a la luz de los luceros,
en el establo caliente
que sabe a madre y a heno.
Y detrás de las carretas,
caminan los carreteros,
con la aijada sobre el hombro
y los ojos en el cielo.
  ¡Cómo lloran las carretas,
camino de Pueblo Nuevo!
  En la paz del campo, van
dejando los troncos muertos
un olor fresco y honrado
a corazón descubierto.
Y cae el ángelus desde
la torre del pueblo viejo,
sobre los campos talados,
que huelen a cementerio.
  ¡Cómo lloran las carretas,
camino de Pueblo Nuevo!

"THE LUMBER WAGONS"

The lumber wagons are already there.
—The pines and the wind have told us,
the golden moon has told us,
the smoke and the echo have told us . . .
They are the carts that go by
in these afternoons at dusk,
the lumber wagons carrying
the dead trees down from the mountain.
What a sound of crying from these carts
on the road to Pueblo Nuevo!
The oxen come along
in the starlight, daydreaming
about their warm stalls in the barn
smelling of motherhood and hay.
And behind the lumber wagons
the ox-drivers walking,
the ox-prod on their shoulders,
and eyes watching the sky.
What a sound of crying from these carts
on the road to Pueblo Nuevo!
The dead trees as they move
through the calm of the fields
leave behind a fresh honest smell
like a heart thrown open.
The Angelus falls
from the steeple of the ancient town
over the stripped fields
which smell like a cemetery.
What a sound of crying from these carts
on the road to Pueblo Nuevo!

ESTAMPA DE INVIERNO

(Nieve)

¿Dónde se han escondido los colores
en este día negro y blanco?
La fronda, negra; el agua, gris; el cielo
y la tierra, de un blanquinegro pálido;
y la ciudad doliente
una vieja aguafuerte de romántico.

El que camina, negro;
negro el medroso pájaro
que atraviesa el jardín como una flecha . . .
Hasta el silencio es duro y despintado.

La tarde cae. El cielo
no tiene ni un dulzor. En el ocaso,
un vago amarillor casi esplendente,
que casi no lo es. Lejos, el campo
de hierro seco.
                    Y entra la noche, como
un entierro; enlutado
y frío todo, sin estrellas, blanca
y negra, como el día negro y blanco.

WINTER SCENE

(Snow)

Where have the colors all gone to
today, that is so black and white?
The leaves black, the water gray, the sky
and the ground a sort of faded white and black,
and the mournful city
is like an old steel engraving by some romantic.

The man who is walking is black,
the startled bird is black
shooting across the garden like an arrow . . .
Even the silence is harsh and faded.

Dusk falls. There is nothing gentle
about the sky. In the west, an indecisive
yellow light that almost glitters
and almost doesn't. Over there, fields
like dry iron.
                    And the night comes, like
a burial; it is all wrapped in black
and cold, no stars, all white
and black, like the black and white day.

"QUIEN SABE"

¡Quién sabe del revés de cada hora!

¡Cuántas veces la aurora
estaba tras un monte!

¡Cuántas el rejio hervor de un horizonte
tenía en sus entrañas de oro el trueno!

Aquella rosa era veneno.

Aquella espada dio la vida.

Yo pensé una florida
pradera en el remate de un camino,
y me encontré un pantano.

Yo soñaba en la gloria de lo humano,
y me hallé en lo divino.

"WHO KNOWS WHAT IS GOING ON"

Who knows what is going on on the other side of
each hour?

How many times the sunrise was
there, behind a mountain!

How many times the brilliant cloud piling up far off
was already a golden body full of thunder!

This rose was poison.

That sword gave life.

I was thinking of a flowery meadow
at the end of a road,
and found myself in the slough.

I was thinking of the greatness of what was human,
and found myself in the divine.

"EL RECUERDO SE VA"

El recuerdo se va
por mi memoria larga, removiendo
con finos pies las hojas secas.

—Detrás, la casa está vacía.
Delante, carreteras
que llevan a otras partes, solas,
yertas.
Y la lluvia que llora ojos y ojos,
cual si la hora eterna se quedase ciega.—

Aunque la casa está muda y cerrada,
yo, aunque no estoy en ella, estoy en ella.
Y . . . ¡adiós, tú que caminas
sin volver la cabeza!

"A REMEMBRANCE IS MOVING"

A remembrance is moving
down the long memory, disturbing
the dry leaves with its delicate feet.

—Behind, the house is empty.
On ahead, highways
going on to other places, solitary highways,
stretched out.
And the rain is like weeping eyes,
as if the eternal moment were going blind—.

Even though the house is quiet and shut,
even though I am not in it, I am in it.
And . . . good-bye, you who are walking
without turning your head!

"EL CORDERO BALABA DULCEMENTE"

El cordero balaba dulcemente.
El asno, tierno, se alegraba
en un llamar caliente.
El perro ladreaba,
hablando casi a las estrellas . . .
Me desvelé. Salí. Vi huellas
celestes por el suelo
florecido
como un cielo
invertido.
Un vaho tibio y blando
velaba la arboleda;
la luna iba declinando
en un ocaso de oro y seda,
que parecía un ámbito divino . . .
Mi pecho palpitaba,
como si el corazón tuviese vino . . .
Abrí el establo a ver si estaba
El allí.
¡ Estaba!

The lamb was bleating softly.
The young jackass grew happier
with his excited bray.
The dog barked,
almost talking to the stars.
    I woke up! I went out. I saw the tracks
of the sky on the ground
which had flowered
like a sky
turned upside down.
    A warm and mild haze
hung around the trees;
the moon was going down
in a west of gold and silk
like some full and divine womb . . .
    My chest was thumping
as if my heart were drunk . . .
    I opened the barn door to see if
He was there.
            He was!

RETORNO FUGAZ

¿Cómo era, Dios mío, cómo era?
—¡Oh, corazón falaz, mente indecisa!—
¿Era como el pasaje de la brisa?
¿Como la huída de la primavera?

Tan leve, tan voluble, tan lijera
cual estival vilano . . . ¡Sí! Imprecisa
como sonrisa que se pierde en risa . . .
¡Vana en el aire, igual que una bandera!

¡Bandera, sonreír, vilano, alada
primavera de junio, brisa pura! . . .
¡Qué loco fué tu carnaval, qué triste!

Todo tu cambiar trocóse en nada
—¡memoria, ciega abeja de amargura!—
¡No sé cómo eras, yo que sé que fuiste!

RETURN FOR AN INSTANT

What was it like, God of mine, what was it like?
—Oh unfaithful heart, indecisive intelligence!
Was it like the going by of the wind?
Like the disappearance of the spring?

As nimble, as changeable, as weightless
as milkweed seeds in summer . . . Yes! Indefinite
as a smile which is lost forever in a laugh . . .
Arrogant in the air, just like a flag!

Flag, smile, milkweed pod, swift
spring in June, clear wind! . . .
Your celebration was so wild, so sad!

All of your changes ended up in nothing—
remembrance, a blind bee of bitter things!—
I don't know what you were like, but you were!

from

Diary of a Poet
Recently Married

(Diario de un Poeta Recién Casado)
1916

"QUE CERCA YA DEL ALMA"

¡Qué cerca ya del alma
lo que está tan inmensamente lejos
de las manos aún!

Como una luz de estrella,
como una voz sin nombre
traída por el sueño, como el paso
de algún corcel remoto
que oímos, anhelantes,
el oído en la tierra;
como el mar en teléfono . . .

Y se hace la vida
por dentro, con la luz inestinguible
de un día deleitoso
que brilla en otra parte.

¡Oh, qué dulce, qué dulce
verdad sin realidad aún, qué dulce!

"SOMETHING SO CLOSE"

Something so close to the soul
though still so enormously far
from the hands!

Like the light from a star,
like a voice we cannot identify
in a dream, like the galloping
of some rider far off
which we listen to, holding our breath,
our ear touching the ground,
like the sea over the telephone . . .

And life takes place
inside us, with the eternal light
of an ecstatic day
which is going on somewhere else.

It is a beautiful thing,
something true and not yet real, beautiful!

NOCTURNO

¡Oh mar sin olas conocidas,
sin "estaciones" de parada,
agua y luna, no más, noches y noches!

. . . Me acuerdo de la tierra,
que, ajena, era de uno,
al pasarla en la noche de los trenes,
por los lugares mismos y a las horas
de otros años . . .

          —Madre lejana,
tierra dormida,
de brazos firmes y constantes,
de igual regazo quieto
—tumba de vida eterna
con el mismo ornamento renovado—;
tierra madre, que siempre
aguardas en tu sola
verdad el mirar triste
de los errantes ojos!—

        . . . Me acuerdo de la tierra
—los olivares a la madrugada—,
firme frente a la luna
blanca, rosada o amarilla,
esperando retornos y retornos
de los que, sin ser suyos ni sus **dueños**,
la amaron y la amaron . . .

NIGHT PIECE

The sea with no waves we recognize,
with no stations on its route,
only water and moon, night after night!

My thought goes back to the land,
someone else's land, belonging to the one
going through it on trains at night,
through the same place at the same hour
as before . . .

        Remote mother,
sleeping earth,
powerful and faithful arms,
the same quiet lap for all
—tomb of eternal life
with the same decorations freshened—
earth, mother, always
true to yourself, waiting for
the sad gaze
of the wandering eyes!

My thought goes back to the land,
—the olive groves at sunrise—
outlined sharply in the white
or golden or yellow moonlight,
that look forward to the coming back
of those humans who are neither its slaves nor its
        masters,
but who love it anyway . . .

"TE DESHOJE, COMO UNA ROSA"

Te deshojé, como una rosa,
para verte tu alma,
y no la vi.

Mas todo en torno
—horizontes de tierras y de mares—,
todo, hasta el infinito,
se colmó de una esencia
inmensa y viva.

"I TOOK OFF PETAL AFTER PETAL"

I took off petal after petal, as if you were a rose,
in order to see your soul,
and I didn't see it.

However, everything around—
horizons of fields and oceans—
everything, even what was infinite,
was filled with a perfume,
immense and living.

New York,
28 de marzo

CEMENTERIO

Se ha quedado esta pequeña aldea de muertos, olvido que se recordara, al amor de unos árboles que fueron grandes en su niñez agreste, pequeños, hoy que son viejos, entre los terribles rascacielos. La noche deja, ahora, paralelos los vivos que duermen, un poco más alto, con los muertos que duermen, un poco más abajo, hace un poco más de tiempo y para un poco más de tiempo. ¡Paralelos hacia un infinito cercano en el que no se encontrarán!

Quita el viento y pone, cegándome de un agudo blandor, la nieve—que se irisa en sus altos remolinos, a la luz de las farolas blancas—, de las tumbas. Las horas agudizan la sombra, y lo que descansó en la luz del día, está despierto, y mira, escucha y ve. Así, los sueños de estos muertos se oyen, como si ellos soñaran alto, y su soñar de tantos años, más vivo que el soñar de los muertos de una noche, es la vida más alta y más honda de la ciudad desierta.

New York,
March 28th

CEMETERY

This tiny village of dead people has stayed on, forgetfulness which is remembered, in the care of some trees that in their rural childhood were large, and now that they are old, are small, among the frightening skyscrapers. Now the night makes the living who are asleep a little higher up, parallel with the dead who are asleep a little lower down, a little time that is past and a little time to come. Parallel rows toward a neighborly infinity, though in it they will never meet!

The wind removes and puts back the snow, from the gravestones, blinding me with its sharp whiteness, changing colors in its high whirling columns in the light of the white streetlamps. The hours make the darkness more apparent, and whatever was resting in the daylight is awake now, and looks, listens, and sees. In this way the dreams of these dead people are heard, as if they were dreaming out loud, and their dreaming over so many years, more alive than the dreaming of these dead for one night, is the life that is highest and deepest in the abandoned city.

"EN SUBWAY"

En subway. La sufragista, de una fealdad alardeada, con su postre mustio por sombrero, se levanta hacia un ancianito rojo que entra, y le ofrece, con dignidad imperativa, su sitio. El se resiste, mirando con humildad celeste a la nieve entre dos sombreros de señoras negras. Ella le coge por el brazo. El se indigna, en una actitud de quita golpes. Ella lo sienta, sin hablar, de una vez. El se queda hablando sin voz, agitando furioso las manos altas, con una chispa de sangre última en sus claros y débiles ojos azules.

New York,
April 2nd

"IN THE SUBWAY"

In the subway. The suffragette, with an ugliness that is positively exhibitionistic, and some stale pastry for a hat, rises toward a red-faced old man who comes in and, with a domineering dignity, offers him her seat. He resists, looking with divine humility at the snow between two Negro women's hats. She takes him by the arm. He becomes indignant and looks as though he might hit someone. She sits him down, once and for all, without speaking. He goes on talking soundlessly, moving his raised hands furiously, a final spark of blood in his clear eyes that are weak and blue.

ALTA NOCHE

New York solitario ¡sin cuerpo! . . . Y voy despacio, Quinta Avenida abajo, cantando alto. De vez en cuando, me paro a contemplar los enormes y complicados cierres de los bancos, los escaparates en transformación, las banderolas ondeantes en la noche . . . Y este eco, que, como dentro de un aljibe inmenso, ha venido en mi oído inconsciente, no sé desde qué calle, se acerca, se endurece, se ancha. Son unos pasos claudicantes y arrastrados como por el cielo, que llegan siempre y no acaban de llegar. Me paro una vez más y miro arriba y abajo. Nada. La luna ojerosa de primavera mojada, el eco y yo.

De pronto, no sé si cerca o lejos, como aquel carabinero solitario por las playas de Castilla, aquella tarde de vendaval, un punto, un niño, un animal, un enano . . . ¿Qué? Y avanza. ¡Ya! . . . Casi no pasa junto a mí. Entonces vuelvo la cara y me encuentro con la mirada suya, brillante, negra, roja y amarilla, mayor que el rostro, todo y solo él. Y un negro viejo, cojo, de paletó mustio y sombrero de copa mate, me saluda ceremonioso y sonriente, y sigue, Quinta Avenida arriba . . . Me recorre un breve escalofrío, y, las manos en los bolsillos, sigo, con la luna amarilla en la cara, semicantando.

El eco del negro cojo, rey de la ciudad, va dando la vuelta a la noche por el cielo, ahora hacia el poniente . . .

DEEP NIGHT

New York deserted—without a person! I walk down Fifth Avenue, with lots of time, singing aloud. From time to time, I stop to look at the gigantic and complicated locks in the banks, the department store windows being changed, the flags flapping in the night . . . And this sound which my ears, as if inside some enormous cistern, have taken in unconsciously, coming from I don't know which street, gets nearer, harder, louder. The sounds are footsteps, shuffling and limping, they seem to be coming from above, they constantly approach and never manage to get here. I stop again and look up the avenue and down. Nothing. The moist spring moon, with circles under its eyes, the sounds, and I.

Suddenly, I can't tell if far off or near, like the solitary soldier I saw on the sands of Castille, that evening when the sea wind was strong, a point or a child, or an animal, or a dwarf—What? And slowly it comes closer. Closer. About to pass. I turn my face and meet his gaze, the eyes bright, black, red and yellow, larger than his face, all he is is his gaze. An old Negro, crippled, with a shrunken overcoat and a hat with a faded top, greets me ceremoniously, and then, smiling, goes on up Fifth Avenue . . . A brief shudder goes through me, and with my hands in my pockets I go on, the yellow moon in my face, half singing to myself.

The echo of the crippled Negro, king of the city, makes a turn around the night in the sky, now toward the west.

AUTHOR'S CLUB

Creí siempre que en New York pudiera no haber poetas. Lo que no sospechaba es que hubiese tantos poetas malos, ni un tugurio como éste, tan seco y polvoriento como nuestro Ateneo Madrileño, a pesar de estar en un piso 15, casi a la altura del Parnaso.

Son señores de décima clase, que cultivan parecidos físicos a Poe, a Walt Whitman, a Stevenson, a Mark Twain, y que se dejan consumir el alma con su cigarro gratuito, hechos uno con él; melenudos que se ríen de Robinson, de Frost, de Masters, de Vachel Lindsay, de Amy Lowell, y que no se ríen de Poe, de Emily Dickinson y de Whitman, porque ya están muertos. Y me muestran paredes y paredes llenas de retratos y autógrafos en barquillo, de Bryant, de Aldrich, de Lowell, de, de, de . . .

. . . He cogido de la fumadora un cigarrillo y, encendiéndolo, lo he echado en un rincón, sobre la alfombra, a ver si el fuego se levanta y deja, en vez de este Club de escoria, un alto hueco fresco y hondo, con estrellas claras, en el cielo limpio de la noche de abril.

AUTHOR'S CLUB

I had always thought perhaps there would be no poets at all in New York. What I had never suspected was that there would be so many bad ones, or a place like this, as dry and dusty as our own Ateneo in Madrid, in spite of its being on the 15th floor, almost at the altitude of Parnassus.

Tenth-rate men, all of them, cultivating physical resemblances to Poe, to Walt Whitman, to Stevenson, to Mark Twain, letting their soul be burned up with their free cigar, since the two are the same; bushy-haired men who make fun of Robinson, Frost, Masters, Vachel Lindsay, Amy Lowell and who fail to make fun of Poe, Emily Dickinson and Whitman only because they are already dead. And they show me wall after wall of portraits and autographs in holograph, of Bryant, of Aldrich, of Lowell, etc., etc., etc. . .

. . . I have taken a cigarette from the fumidor, lighted it and thrown it into a corner, on the rug, in order to see if the fire will catch and leave behind it in place of this club of rubbish a high and empty hole, fresh and deep, with clear stars, in the cloudless sky of this April night.

WALT WHITMAN

—Pero, ¿de veras quiere usted ver la casa de Whitman mejor que la de Roosevelt? ¡Nadie me ha pedido nunca tal cosa ...!

... La casa es pequeña y amarilla, y está junto a la vía férrea, como la casa de un gaurdaagujas, en una praderita verde limitada de piedrecillas con cal, bajo un solo árbol. En torno, al llano inmenso so ofrece al viento, que lo barre y nos barre, y deja mondo el mármol tosco y humilde que le dice a los trenes:

TO MARK THE BIRTHPLACE OF

WALT WHITMAN

THE GOOD GRAY POET

BORN MAY 31, 1819

ERECTED BY THE COLONIAL SOCIETY

OF HUNTINGTON IN 1905

Como el estanciero no parece que está, doy vueltas a la casa, intentando ver algo por sus ventanuchos ... De pronto, un hombre alto, lento y barbudo, en camisa y con sombrero ancho, como el retrato juvenil de Whitman, viene—¿de dónde?—y me dice, apoyado en su barra de hierro, que no sabe quién es Whitman, que él es polaco, que la casa es suya y que no tiene ganas de enseñársela a nadie. Y, encojiéndose, se mete dentro, por la puertecita que parece de juguete.

Soledad y frío. Pasa un tren, contra el viento. El sol, grana un instante, se muere tras el bosque bajo, y en la charca verde y un poco sangrienta que bordeamos, silban, en el silencio enorme, innumerables sapos.

WALT WHITMAN

"But do you really want to see Whitman's house instead of Roosevelt's? I've never had this request before!"

The house is tiny and yellow, and next to the railroad track, like the hut of a switchman, in a small green patch of grass, marked out with whitewashed stones, beneath a single tree. Around it, the wide meadow area is open to the wind, which sweeps it, and us, and has polished the simple rough piece of marble which announces to the trains:

TO MARK THE BIRTHPLACE OF
WALT WHITMAN
THE GOOD GRAY POET
BORN MAY 31, 1819
ERECTED BY THE COLONIAL SOCIETY
OF HUNTINGTON IN 1905

Since the farmer doesn't seem to be at home, I walk around the house a couple of times, hoping to see something through the windowlets. Suddenly a man, tall, slow-moving and bearded, wearing a shirt and wide-brimmed hat—like the early photograph of Whitman—comes, from somewhere, and tells me, leaning on his iron bar, that he doesn't know who Whitman was, that he is Polish, that this house is his, and that he does not intend to show it to anyone. Then pulling himself up, he goes inside, through the little door that looks like a toy door.

Solitude and cold. A train goes by, into the wind. The sun, scarlet for an instant, dies behind the low woods, and in the swamp we walk past which is green and faintly blood-colored, innumerable toads are croaking in the enormous silence.

43

UN IMITADOR DE BILLY SUNDAY

Billy Sunday, el terrible predicador, no se atreve a venir a esta "Ciudad de incrédulos". Pero tiene discípulos de una "fuerza" relativa. Así este Pastor A. Ray Petty, de la Iglesia Anabaptista de Washington Square. He aquí dos de sus anuncios:

Anuncio en "C":

CRISIS DEL CRISTO

Recital de órgano, a las 7,45 de la tarde

Sermón, a las 8 de la tarde

FUNCIONES ESPECIALES EL DOMINGO POR LA NOCHE

A. RAY PETTY

Temas:

Abril 2. Cristo y la caterva

Abril 9. Cristo y el cobarde

Abril 16. Cristo y la cruz

Abril 23. Cristo y la conquista

Abril 30. Cristo y la corona

MÚSICA EXTRAORDINARIA   BUEN CANTO

BIENVENIDO SEAS

Anuncio en "Sportsman":

SERMONES DE BASEBALL

Los domingos por la noche, a las 8

A. Ray Petty, Pastor

Temas:

Mayo 14. "El Pala" en aprieto

Mayo 21. Golpe sacrificado

Mayo 28. Se supende el juego a causa de la oscuridad

MENSAJES DE VIDA   ACABADOS DE SALIR DE LA PALA

44

AN IMITATOR OF BILLY SUNDAY

Billy Sunday, the fear-inspiring preacher, does not dare to come to this "city of heathens." However, he has disciples with a certain relative "power." One of these is Pastor A. Ray Petty, of the Anabaptist Church in Washington Square. Here are two of his public announcements:

Notice in "C":

THE CRISES OF CHRIST
Organ recital 7:45 P.M.

Preaching 8 P.M.

SPECIAL SUNDAY EVENING SERVICES

A. RAY PETTY

Topics:

April	2.	Christ and the crowd
April	9.	Christ and the coward
April	16.	Christ and the cross
April	23.	Christ and the conquest
April	30.	Christ and the crown

SPECIAL MUSIC   GOOD SINGING

YOU ARE WELCOME

Notice in "Sportsman":

BASEBALL SERMONS
Sunday evening at 8 P.M.

A. Ray Petty, Pastor

Topics:

May 14.	The pinch hitter
May 21.	The sacrifice hit
May 28.	Game called on account of darkness

LIVE MESSAGES   HOT OFF THE BAT

. . . Es noche de primavera. La plaza, verde; el cielo, un poco dorado aún del día caliente y polvoriento; la luna, como un pájaro de luz, de árbol a árbol; el aire, húmedo de los surtidores desflecados por el viento fuerte y grato. Parece la plaza el gran patio de una casa de vecinos. En los bancos, gente sórdida, que duerme en fraternal desahogo. Borrachos, borrachos, borrachos hablando con niños, con la luna, con quien pasa . . . De Mac-Dougal Alley vienen musiquillas y gritos de la gente que se ve bailar en las casas abiertas. La iglesia también está de par en par. Entran en ella los gritos de los niños y salen de ella los gritos del pastor semiterrible que, sin cuello, se desgañita en su sermón—sudor y gesto—de frontón.

A spring night. Washington Square green, the sky still faintly gold from the day which was hot and dusty; the moon moves like a bird made of the light from tree to tree; the air is moist from jets of water whose tips are sheared off by the gusty and welcome wind. The Square looks like a tenement courtyard. Tumbledown people are asleep on the benches in a friendly forgiveness of each other. And drunks, drunks, drunks, talking to children, to the moon, to everyone going by . . . Bursts of music can be heard from MacDougal Alley, and voices of dancers from the houses with open doors. The church also stands wide open. Into it go the cries of the street children, and out of it come the cries of the half fear-inspiring pastor, who is throwing himself about now, his collar off, sweating and waving his arms, in his baseball sermon.

DESHORA

"Abingdon Sq." Dos de la madrugada. Una farola de cristal negro con letras encendidas en blanco:

INASMUCH MISSION
(Misión con motivo de . . .)
SERVICES AT 8 P.M.

Entre dos escaparates de probres y aislados grapefruits y to-mates, cuyos amarillos y carmines duermen un poco, tristes, hasta mañana, una escalerilla sucia baja a una puerta humilde. Todo en dos metros de espacio y encuadrado, como esquelas de de-función, en madera de luto con polvo. Y en un cristal de la puerta, con luz:

WHAT MUST I DO TO BE SAVED?

Come and hear

REV. L. R. CARTER

(¿Qué he de hacer para salvarme?
Ven a oír al Rev. L. R. C.)

WRONG TIME

"Abingdon Square." Two o'clock in the morning. A sign made of black glass with letters lit up in white:

INASMUCH MISSION
SERVICES AT 8:00 P.M.

Between two storefronts of poor and lonesome grapefruits, and tomatoes, whose yellows and scarlets are sleeping a little, sadly, until tomorrow, a sad and dirty stair goes down to an unpretentious door. The whole thing six feet wide and framed, like death notices, in wood turned funereal from dust. And in a glass panel of the door, lighted:

WHAT MUST I DO TO BE SAVED?
Come and hear
REV. L. R. CARTER

49

"ANDAN POR NEW YORK"

Andan por New York, mala amiga—¿por qué?—de Boston, la culta, la Ciudad-Eje, unos versillos que dicen así:

> Here is to good old Boston,
> the home of the bean and the cod,
> where the Cabots speak only to Lowells,
> and the Lowells speak only to God.

He conocido bien a una Cabot. ¡Cómo deben de aburrirse los Lowells! He leído *La fuente* de Lowell. ¡Cómo debe de estarse aburriendo Dios!

"IN NEW YORK"

In New York, which is a bad friend—don't ask me why—of Boston, the cultivated city, the Hub, there are some verses going around like this:

> Here is to good old Boston,
> the home of the bean and the cod,
> where the Cabots speak only to Lowells,
> and the Lowells speak only to God.

I know one of the Cabot women well. How bored the Lowells must be! I read "The Fountain" by Lowell. How bored God must be!

CRISTALES MORADOS
Y MUSELINAS BLANCAS

¡Cristales morados! . . . son como una ejecutoria de hidalguía. Hay muchos en Boston y algunos en New York, por el barrio viejo de Washington Square, ¡tan grato, tan acogedor, tan silencioso! En la Ciudad-Eje especialmente, estos cristales bellos perduran y se cuidan con un altivo celo egoísta.

Son de la época colonial. En su fabricación se emplearon sustancias que, con el sol de los años, han ido tornándolos del color de la amatista, del pensamiento, de la violeta. Parece que por ellos se viese, entre las dulces muselinas blancas de sus mismas casas en paz, el alma fina y noble de aquellos días de plata y oro verdaderos, sin sonido material.

Como las flores y las piedras que antes dije, los hay que tienen casi imperceptible el tono, y hay que hacer habilidades para vérselo; otros, lo dan vagamente, cuando los pasa el sol, las tardes de ocaso puro, en las muselinas blancas, sus hermanas; otros, en fin, son ya morados del todo, podridos de nobleza.

Con ellos sí está mi corazón, América, como una violeta, una amatista o un pensamiento, envuelto en la nieve de las muselinas. Te lo he ido sembrando, en reguero dulce, al pie de las magnolias que se ven en ellos, para que, cada abril, las flores rosas y blancas sorprendan con aroma el retorno vespertino o nocturno de las sencillas puritanas de traje liso, mirada noble y trenzas de oro gris, que tornen, suaves, a su hogar de aquí, en las serenas horas primaverales de terrena nostaljia.

LAVENDER WINDOWPANES
AND WHITE CURTAINS

Lavender windowpanes! They are like a pedigree of nobility. Boston has many of them and New York has a few, in the old streets around Washington Square, so pleasing, so hospitable, so full of silence! These beautiful panes survive particularly in Boston and are cared for with a haughty, self-interested zeal.

They go back to colonial days. The panes were made with substances which the sunlight over the years has been turning the color of the amethyst, of pansies, of the violet. One feels sure that between the sweet white muslin curtains of those quiet houses, he could glimpse through the violet pane the frail and noble spirit of those days, days of genuine silver and genuine gold, making no hearable sound.

Some of the panes have their violet color almost invisibly, like the flowers and stones I spoke of, and it takes skill simply to see it; others transfer their vague shading to their sister curtains, when the light of the pure sunsets strikes them; finally, by now a few panes are lavender all through, rotten with nobility.

My heart lingers back there with these panes, America, like an amethyst, a pansy, a violet, in the center of the muslin snow. I have been planting that heart for you in the ground beneath the magnolias that the panes reflect, so that each April the pink and white flowers and their odor will surprise the simple puritan women with their plain clothes, their noble look, and their pale gold hair, coming back at evening, quietly returning to their homes here in those calm spring hours that have made them homesick for earth.

New York,
cuarto vacío, entre baúles cerrados,
6 de junio, noche

REMORDIMIENTO

Le taparía el tiempo
con rosas, porque no
recordara.

Una rosa distinta,
de una imprevista majia,
sobre cada hora solitaria de oro
o sombra,
hueco propicio a las memorias trájicas.

Que, como entre divinas
y alegres
enredaderas rosas, granas, blancas,
que no dejaran sitio a lo pasado,
se le enredara,
con el cuerpo,
el alma.

New York,
room empty, among closed trunks,
June 6th, at night

REMORSE

Time must have covered it over
with roses so
it would not be remembered.

One particular rose,
that has an unexpected magic,
on top of each lonely hour of gold
or shadows,
a place just right to hold painful memories.

So that among the divine
and joyful
climbing roses, scarlet, white,
which would leave no room for the past,
the soul would be
wound into
the body.

NOCTURNO

El barco, lento y raudo a un tiempo, vence el agua,
mas no al cielo.
Lo azul se queda atrás, abierto en plata viva,
y está otra vez delante.
Fijo, el mástil se mece y torna siempre
—como un horario en igual hora
de la esfera—
a las mismas estrellas,
hora tras hora azul y negra.
El cuerpo va, soñando,
a la tierra que˙es de él, de la otra tierra
que no es de él. El alma queda y sigue
siempre por su dominio eterno.

June 18th

NIGHT PIECE

The ship, slow and rushing at the same time, can
    get ahead of the water
but not the sky.
The blue is left behind, opened up in living silver,
and is ahead of us again.
The mast, fixed, swings and constantly returns
—like an hour hand that points
always to the same hour—
to the same stars,
hour after hour black and blue.
The body as it daydreams goes
toward the earth that belongs to it, from the other earth
that does not. The soul stays on board, moving
through the kingdom it has owned from birth.

from

Later Poems

"INTELIJENCIA, DAME"

¡Intelijencia, dame
el nombre exacto de las cosas!
. . . Que mi palabra sea
la cosa misma,
creada por mi alma nuevamente.
Que por mí vayan todos
los que no las conocen, a las cosas;
que por mí vayan todos
los que ya las olvidan, a las cosas;
que por mí vayan todos
los mismos que las aman, a las cosas . . .
¡Intelijencia, dame
el nombre exacto, y tuyo,
y suyo, y mío, de las cosas!

"INTELLIGENCE, GIVE ME"

Intelligence, give me
the exact name of things!
. . . I want my word to be
the thing itself,
created by my soul a second time.
So that those who do not know them
can go to the things through me,
all those who have forgotten them
can go to the things through me,
all those who love them
can go to the things through me . . .
Intelligence, give me
the exact name, and your name
and theirs and mine, for things!

MARES

¡Siento que el barco mío
ha tropezado, allá en el fondo,
con algo grande!
                    ¡Y nada
sucede! Nada . . . Quietud . . . Olas . . .

—¿Nada sucede; o es que ha sucedido todo,
y estamos ya, tranquilos, en lo nuevo?—

OCEANS

I have a feeling that my boat
has struck, down there in the depths,
against a great thing.
                    And nothing
happens! Nothing . . . Silence . . . Waves . . .

—Nothing happens? Or has everything happened,
and are we standing now, quietly, in the new life?

"LA MUSICA"

¡La música;
—mujer desnuda,
corriendo loca por la noche pura!—

"MUSIC"

Music—
a naked woman
running mad through the pure night!

"COBRE LA RIENDA"

Cobré la rienda,
di la vuelta al caballo
del alba;
me entré, blanco, en la vida.

¡Oh, cómo me miraban,
locas,
las flores de mi sueño,
levantando los brazos a la luna!

"I PULLED ON THE REINS"

I pulled on the reins,
I turned the horse
of the dawn,
and I came in to life, pale.

Oh how they looked at me,
the flowers of my dream,
insane,
lifting their arms to the moon!

A DANTE

Allegro sì, che appena
il conoscìa . . . —DANTE

Tu soneto, lo mismo
que una mujer desnuda y casta,
sentándome en sus piernas puras,
me abrazó con sus brazos celestiales.

Soñé, después, con él, con ella.
Era una fuente
que dos chorros arqueaba en una taza
primera, la cual, luego, los vertía,
finos, en otras dos . . .

TO DANTE

Allegro sì, che appena
il conoscìa . . . —DANTE

Your sonnet, just like
some pure and naked woman,
seated me on her chaste knees,
put her heavenly arms around me.

Afterwards, I dreamt of it, and of her.
                            I saw a fountain
that arched two streams down into a basin,
the first, and then from it two others poured,
more delicate . . .

EL RECUERDO

¡Oh recuerdos secretos,
fuera de los caminos
de todos los recuerdos!

¡Recuerdos, que una noche,
de pronto, resurjís,
como una rosa en un desierto,
como una estrella al mediodía,
—pasión mayor del frío olvido—,
jalones de la vida
mejor de uno,
que casi no se vive!

          ¡Senda
diariamente árida;
maravilla, de pronto,
de primavera única,
de los recuerdos olvidados!

THE MEMORY

Secret memories
not on the road
of our other memories!

Memories, that one night,
suddenly, come alive,
like a rose in the desert,
like a star at noon,
—the stronger burning in this cold nothingness—
landmarks of the best
life a man has,
which is hardly lived at all!

Path dry
day after day;
then the miracle, suddenly,
an amazing springtime,
memories returned from the past!

DESVELO

Se va la noche, negro toro
—plena carne de luto, de espanto y de misterio—;
que ha bramado terrible, inmensamente,
al temor sudoroso de todos los caídos;
y el día viene, niño fresco,
pidiendo confianza, amor y risa,
—niño que, allá muy lejos,
en los arcanos donde
se encuentran los comienzos con los fines,
ha jugado un momento,
por no sé qué pradera
de luz y sombra,
con el toro que huía—.

BEING AWAKE

Night goes away, a black bull—
body heavy with mourning and fear and mystery—
it has been bellowing horribly, monstrously,
in genuine fear of all the dead;
and day arrives, a young child
who wants trust, and love, and jokes,
—a child who somewhere
far away, in the secret places
where what ends meets what is starting,
has been playing a moment
on some meadow or other
of light and darkness
with that bull who is running away . . .

RUTA

Todos duermen, abajo.
                              Arriba, alertas,
el timonel y yo.

El, mirando la aguja, dueño de
los cuerpos, con sus llaves
echadas. Yo, los ojos
en lo infinito, guiando
los tesoros abiertos de las almas.

ROAD

They all are asleep, below.

                         Above, awake,
the helmsman and I.

He, watching the compass needle, lord
of the bodies, with their keys turned
in the locks. I, with my eyes
toward the infinite, guiding
the open treasures of the souls.

"YO NO SOY YO"

Yo no soy yo.
              Soy este
que va a mi lado sin yo verlo;
que, a veces, voy a ver,
y que, a veces, olvido.
El que calla, sereno, cuando hablo,
el que perdona, dulce, cuando odio,
el que pasea por donde no estoy,
el que quedará en pie cuando yo muera.

"I AM NOT I"

I am not I.
                    I am this one
walking beside me whom I do not see,
whom at times I manage to visit,
and whom at other times I forget;
who remains calm and silent while I talk,
and forgives, gently, when I hate,
who walks where I am not,
who will remain standing when I die.

"EL BARCO ENTRA, OPACO Y NEGRO"

El barco entra, opaco y negro,
en la negrura trasparente
del puerto inmenso.
                              Paz y frío.
                                        —Los que esperan,
están aún dormidos con su sueño,
tibios en ellos, lejos todavía y yertos dentro de él
de aquí, quizás . . .

   ¡Oh vela real nuestra, junto al sueño
de duda de los otros! ¡Seguridad, al lado
del sueño inquieto por nosotros!—
                              Paz. Silencio.
Silencio que al romperse, con el alba,
hablará de otro modo . . .

"THE SHIP, SOLID AND BLACK"

The ship, solid and black,
enters the clear blackness
of the great harbor.
                    Quiet and cold.
                              —The people waiting
are still asleep, dreaming,
and warm, far away and still stretched out in this
dream, perhaps . . .

How real our watch is, beside the dream
of doubt the others had! How sure it is, compared
to their troubled dream about us!
                         Quiet. Silence.
Silence which in breaking up at dawn
will speak differently.

"TAN BIEN COMO SE ENCUENTRA"

¡Tan bien como se encuentra
mi alma en mi cuerpo
—como una idea única
en su verso perfecto—,
y que tenga que irse y que dejar
el cuerpo—como el verso de un retórico—
vano y yerto!

BLANCOR

Olor de nardo,
mujer desnuda
por los oscuros corredores.

"EVEN THOUGH MY SOUL"

Even though my soul fits so wonderfully
inside my body—
like a clear idea
in a line perfect for it—
nevertheless it has to abandon the body
eventually, leaving it like some academic's line,
hollow and stiff!

WHITENESS

Fragrance of spikenard,
a naked woman
in the dark corridors.

LUNA GRANDE

La puerta está abierta;
el grillo, cantando.
¿Andas tú desnuda
por el campo?

Como un agua eterna,
por todo entra y sale.
¿Andas tú desnuda
por el aire?

La albahaca no duerme,
la hormiga trabaja.
¿Andas tú desnuda
por la casa?

FULL MOON

The door is open,
the cricket singing.
Are you going around naked
in the fields?

Like an immortal water,
going in and out of everything.
Are you going around naked
in the air?

The basil is not asleep,
the ant is busy.
Are you going around naked
in the house?

"VINO, PRIMERO, PURA"

Vino, primero, pura,
vestida de inocencia.
Y la amé como un niño.

Luego se fue vistiendo
de no sé qué ropajes.
Y la fui odiando, sin saberlo.

Llegó a ser una reina,
fastuosa de tesoros . . .
¡Qué iracundia de yel y sin sentido!

. . . Mas se fue desnudando.
Y yo le sonreía.

Se quedó con la túnica
de su inocencia antigua.
Creí de nuevo en ella.

Y se quitó la túnica,
y apareció desnuda toda . . .
¡Oh pasión de mi vida, poesía
desnuda, mía para siempre!

"AT FIRST SHE CAME TO ME PURE"

At first she came to me pure,
dressed only in her innocence;
and I loved her as we love a child.

Then she began putting on
clothes she picked up somewhere;
and I hated her, without knowing it.

She gradually became a queen,
the jewelry was blinding . . .
What bitterness and rage!

. . . She started going back toward nakedness.
And I smiled.

Soon she was back to the single shift
of her old innocence.
I believed in her a second time.

Then she took off the cloth
and was entirely naked . . .
Naked poetry, always mine,
that I have loved my whole life!

AURORAS DE MOGUER

¡Los álamos de plata,
saliendo de la bruma!
¡El viento solitario
por la marisma oscura,
moviendo —terremoto
irreal— la difusa
Huelva lejana y rosa!
¡Sobre el mar, por La Rábida,
en la gris perla húmeda
del cielo, aún con la noche
fría tras su alba cruda
—¡horizonte de pinos!—,
fría tras su alba blanca,
la deslumbrada luna!

DAWNS OF MOGUER

The silver poplars
rising out of the fog!
The lonesome wind there
moving over the dark
marsh—an earthquake
that is not real—and Huelva
stretched out, far away, rose-colored!
Above the sea, toward La Rábida,
in the moist pearl-gray
of the sky, with the night
still cold behind its crude dawn—
a horizon of pines—
the baffled moon!

AURORA DE TRASMUROS

A todo se le ve la cara, blanca
—cal, pesadilla, adobe, anemia, frío—
contra el oriente. ¡Oh cerca de la vida;
oh, duro de la vida! ¡Semejanza
animal en el cuerpo—raíz, escoria—
(con el alma mal puesta todavía),
y mineral y vejetal!
¡Sol yerto contra el hombre,
contra el cerdo, las coles y la tapia!
—Falsa alegría, porque estás tan solo
en la hora—se dice—, no en el alma!—

Todo el cielo tomado
por los montones humeantes, húmedos,
de los estercoleros horizontes.
Restos agrios, aquí y allá,
de la noche. Tajadas,
medio comidas, de la luna verde,
cristalitos de estrellas falsas,
papel mal arrancado, con su yeso aún fresco
de cielo azul. Los pájaros,
aún mal despiertos, en la luna cruda,
farol casi apagado.
¡Recua de seres y de cosas!
—¡Tristeza verdadera, porque estás tan solo
en el alma—se dice—, no en la hora!—

DAWN OUTSIDE THE CITY WALLS

You can see the face of everything, and it is
    white—
plaster, nightmare, adobe, anemia, cold—
turned to the east. Oh closeness to life!
Hardness of life! Like something
in the body that is animal—root, slag-ends—
with the soul still not set well there—
and mineral and vegetable!
Sun standing stiffly against man,
against the sow, the cabbages, the mud wall!
—False joy, because you are merely
in time, as they say, and not in the soul!

The entire sky taken up
by moist and steaming heaps,
a horizon of dung piles.
Sour remains, here and there,
of the night. Slices
of the green moon, half-eaten,
crystal bits from false stars,
plaster, the paper ripped off, still faintly
sky-blue. The birds
not really awake yet, in the raw moon,
streetlight nearly out.
Mob of beings and things!
—A true sadness, because you are really deep
in the soul, as they say, not in time at all!

EL NOMBRE CONSEGUIDO DE LOS NOMBRES

Si yo, por ti, he creado un mundo para ti,
dios, tú tenías seguro que venir a él,
y tú has venido a él, a mí seguro,
porque mi mundo todo era mi esperanza.

Yo he acumulado mi esperanza
en lengua, en nombre hablado, en nombre escrito;
a todo yo le había puesto nombre
y tú has tomado el puesto
de toda esta nombradía.

Ahora puedo yo detener ya mi movimiento,
como la llama se detiene en ascua roja
con resplandor de aire inflamado azul,
en el ascua de mi perpetuo estar y ser;
ahora yo soy ya mi mar paralizado,
el mar que yo decía, mas no duro,
paralizado en olas de conciencia en luz
y vivas hacia arriba todas, hacia arriba.

Todos los nombres que yo puse
al universo que por ti me recreaba yo,
se me están convirtiendo en uno y en un
dios.

El dios que es siempre al fin,
el dios creado y recreado y recreado
por gracia y sin esfuerzo.
El Dios. El nombre conseguido de los nombres.

THE NAME DRAWN FROM THE NAMES

If I have created a world for you, in your place,
god, you had to come to it confident,
and you have come to it, to my refuge,
because my whole world was nothing but my hope.

I have been saving up my hope
in language, in a spoken name, a written name;
I had given a name to everything,
and you have taken the place
of all these names.

Now I can hold back my movement
inside the coal of my continual living and being,
as the flame reins itself back inside the red coal,
surrounded by air that is all blue fire;
now I am my own sea that has been suddenly
    stopped somewhere,
the sea I used to speak of, but not heavy,
stiffened into waves of an awareness filled with light,
and all of them moving upward, upward.

All the names that I gave
to the universe that I created again for you
are now all turning into one name, into one
god.

The god who, in the end, is always
the god created and recreated and recreated
through grace and never through force.
The God. The name drawn from the names.

CONCIENCIA PLENA

Tú me llevas, conciencia plena, deseante dios,
por todo el mundo.
                    En este mar tercero,
casi oigo tu voz; tu voz del viento
ocupante total del movimiento;
de los colores, de las luces
eternos y marinos.

Tu voz de fuego blanco
en la totalidad del agua, el barco, el cielo,
lineando las rutas con delicia,
grabándome con fúljido mi órbita segura
de cuerpo negro
con el diamante lúcido en su dentro.

.

92

FULL CONSCIOUSNESS

You are carrying me, full consciousness, god that
    has desires,
all through the world.
                 Here, in this third sea,
I almost hear your voice: your voice, the wind,
filling entirely all movements;
eternal colors and eternal lights,
sea colors and sea lights.

Your voice of white fire
in the universe of water, the ship, the sky,
marking out the roads with delight,
engraving for me with a blazing light my firm orbit:
a black body
with the glowing diamond in its center.

FIRST GLIMPSE OF
JUAN RAMON JIMENEZ

During those exciting years in Madrid, Juan Ramón Jiménez was, to us, even more than Antonio Machado, the man who had raised poetry to the status of a religion, living exclusively because of poetry and for it, dazzling us with his example. In 1924, in *La Verdad*, a literary sheet from Murcia, I published several poems from my *Marinero en tierra* which had not yet appeared in book form. Someone told me that Juan Ramón had liked them very much. I paid him a visit.

He lived on the top floor of a house in a quiet neighborhood, a sort of penthouse. He received me there, among honeysuckles and morning glories which he himself, with his Andalusian homesickness for gardens, was guiding along the walls, and turning into fountains of leaves. That afternoon the writer Antonio Espina was with him.

Juan Ramón was editor at that time of the literary review *Indice* and of a publishing house as well with the same name. Two books had just come out: *Signario*, by Antonio Espina, and Pedro Salinas' *Presagios*. In his apartment, holding a copy of *Signario*, he complained about its typographical imperfections. He had found errata, smudged letters, sloping lines, and over all of this he would lose sleep.

"In Alfonso Reyes' edition of Góngora's *Fábula de Polifemo y Galatea* he let some errata slip by him too: instead of 'corona' there is 'corna'; for 'entre', 'enter', and so on. Spain had lost its tradition of great printing. Take a look at this English book. [He showed us a modern edition of Keats.] Look at the fine workmanship, and the grace, the delicacy of the type! I'd like to obtain the same results in the *Indice* books, but that's obviously asking too much."

In those days Juan Ramón's beard was still black and rough;

he had the perfect profile of the Andalusian Arab, and a soft, gloomy voice that sometimes rose into a scratchy falsetto. We talked about writing, and names from his generation came up: Pérez de Ayala, the Machados, Ortega y Gasset . . . During that visit I glimpsed for the first time—later I saw it often, throughout our friendship—the extraordinary Andalusian wit and venom that came out in making fun of people or doing imitations of them. The people I heard him laugh at most—and slander, in his poetic way—were Azorín and Eugenio D'Ors.

"Have you seen the title of Azorín's last book? *El chirrión de los políticos.* [*The Ox Cart of the Politicians.*] 'The Ox Cart!' I received a personally signed copy dedicated to me. Naturally, I went myself, in person, to his house to give it back to him. Azorín lives," he continued, "in one of those houses that reek of the Madrid dish—boiled-meat-and-vegetables mixed with cat piss. He sleeps far far inside a bed whose mosquito netting is decorated with pink ribbons, and he keeps on his night-table an object he considers to be in the most exquisite taste, a plaster of paris Negro painted black, the kind they use to advertise 'La Estrella' coffee, a gift from his constituents when he was congressman for Monovar. No matter how simple the furnishings are, you can always tell a writer by his home."

He broke off his friendship with Pérez de Ayala one day during a visit because Pérez de Ayala had showed him a room with various sausages hanging from the ceiling; for that he never forgave his friend. He noticed in José Ortega y Gasset's home—remember the visitor is Juan Ramón Jiménez, not I—a small Venus de Milo, cast in plaster, on top of a piano, the sort of piece that sells for a few pennies in the square of Cibeles in Madrid. I believe there was also a brass paperweight that undertook to be Don Quixote, and included a desperate Sancho Panza, shouting at the top of his lungs. These details of decoration gave occasion for biting jibes that Juan Ramón aimed at Ortega, using the details as glimpses into Ortega's style and work.

His own home was very different. He and his wife, Zenobia Camprubí, had succeeded in keeping it with a taste and an elegance that were truly simple, natural. When Juan Ramón was working, and during this time he would work twenty-four hours of the day, it was impossible to see him; he turned away his visitors, sometimes refusing to let them in himself. The names of visitors would be conveyed to him by telephone from the porter's lodge. Occasionally the visitor himself would speak:

"This is so and so."

Juan Ramón would answer in a perfectly natural way, from upstairs: "Juan Ramón Jiménez has left me a message that he is out."

In that sought-after solitude, he produced, polished, retouched, reshuffled his work (or his Work, as he tended to call it) back and forth. In that darkroom of poetry, the poet from the country, the poet of purple and yellow sundowns, of walks with his silver burro through the narrow streets of Moguer, worked on with the fervor of a mystic, of a solitary, listening to the circulation of his own blood, drawing out the poetry that rose from it. The poet of *Arias, Pastorales, Jardines lejanos* became at this time, drawing close to the flame of his work, the poet of *Piedra y cielo, Poesía, Belleza, Unidad.*

> *Imaginary wind from the sea!*
> *Street the sailors like—*
> *blue blouse, and against his chest*
> *the chain that works miracles!*

This stanza was from one of the most transparent and lively of Juan Ramón's poems; I had taken two lines from the stanza as an epigraph for a poem I had published in *La Verdad,* one of those he praised so much:

blue blouse, and against his chest
the chain that works miracles!

The welcome Juan Ramón gave me, which was like the welcome he gave all the poets beginning to appear at that time, though he perhaps showed me preference over the others, was encouraging and warm, and inspired in me a faith and a self-confidence I hadn't possessed until then. He asked me to let him see more of my things and so the next day I brought him a group of short poems from which he himself made a selection and published in *SI,* a review of poetry and prose he edited under the pen name of "The Universal Andalusian."

Those first poems of mine were from *Marinero en tierra (Sailor on land)* a book that shortly after was given the National Award for Literature, together with Gerardo Diego's *Versos humanos.* Offering me further proof of his esteem, Juan Ramón Jiménez wrote me the fine letter I have since published as a preface to my poems.

In Buenos Aires now, from my small balcony overlooking the River Plate, here among my red cardinals and my run-down pots of blackened geraniums, my memory goes northwards up the river, and takes me past the image I have of Juan Ramón in Madrid, lively-eyed in his roof-house of honeysuckles and morning glories, to the picture of the present Juan Ramón, a survivor in America of the immense Spanish catastrophe—living brother of Antonio Machado, who was a genuine piece of the earth sacrificed—like Machado he is a master, a wandering magnificent voice of our country.

RAFAEL ALBERTI
Buenos Aires, 1945
translated by
Hardie St. Martin

Selected Poems of
FEDERICO GARCIA LORCA

GARCIA LORCA AND CRETE

Garcia Lorca's poems often begin with a simple and clear line, a line like "When the moon sails out," then unexpectedly a joyful idea appears, the feelings open in surprise, the walls we have put up to keep things in their places collapse, the instincts pour in—it's as if an animal had written many of his stanzas—mandible feelings come, the jokes of children, the most fantastic delicacy, the longings of the monk for the pure moon, above all desire, desire, desire. What we could call desire-energy passes through Lorca's poems as if the lines were clear arteries created for it. Ortega y Gasset said once: "Europe is suffering from a withering of the ability to desire." Americans are weak in the same way. Everywhere we meet people, old and young, who when you ask them if they want this or that smile amiably but can't remember. The word I love best in Lorca is "quiero," which appears again and again: "I love, I want":

> *Green, how I love you, green!*
> *Green wind. Green branches.*
> *The ship on the sea*
> *and the horse on the mountain.*

> . . .

> *I want the water to go on without its bed,*
> *and the wind to go on without its mountain passes.*

> . . .

> *I have shut my balcony door*
> *because I don't want to hear the sobbing.*

> . . .

I want to sleep for half a second,
a second, a minute, a century,
but I want everyone to know that I'm still alive. . . .

. . .

When I am on the roof
what a pure seraphim of fire I want to be and I am!

We all know great poets who write about imagination, or the difficulty of dying, or political systems, or anxiety, but Lorca writes about what he loves, what he takes delight in, what he wants, what he desires, what barren women desire, what water desires, what gypsies desire, what a bull desires just before he dies, what brothers and sisters desire. . . .

Flamenco guitar, after all, is a poetry of desire, and the Spanish adore both Lorca and Antonio Machado, who both write somehow in "cante jondo" (deep song). At the moment I think they prefer Machado, and one difference between them is what happens to the desire-energy. Machado wanted much too, but he didn't get it. His desire-energy drove straight ahead into a stone wall, his young wife died, he ended up teaching French to high-school students who didn't want to learn it, Spain he found to be a nation where "lies are sacred," the Republic he worked for and in was smashed by the right wing. Some adult spirituality prevents him from interpreting these disasters with self-pity. He found all the things that happened to him to be fair. Machado's poetry, from early on, involves not only pleasure, but what Freud called the reality principle. The Spanish respect that. In Lorca you see desire still flying, hurtling through the air, like a tornado, putting new leaves on every tree it touches, writing as if he belonged to Cretan civilization—on whose murals there are no brutal kings, only bluebirds and winged griffins—a desire for intensity as immense as Dickens's characters' desire for food, a psyche so alive it doesn't like or dislike walls but flies over them.

What Garcia Lorca's poetry would have been after Franco's victory we don't know. After all, Lorca died when he was only thirty-seven, shot by an impromptu firing squad, as he was just beginning, in his Ghazals and Casidas, to notice some darkness as he flew about the planet. Interestingly, he adopted old Arab poetic forms to help entangle that union of desire and darkness, which the ancient Arabs loved so much.

II

In 1929, when Lorca was thirty, he grew restless, and came to the United States, where he lived for ten months or so, mostly in a room in John Jay Hall at Columbia. Out of that visit came *The Poet in New York*, which I think is still the greatest book ever written about New York. If we continue the metaphor adopted above, we would have to say that his desire-energy, while still very much alive in the United States, could not find any resonating chambers. It hangs in the air, halfway between his body and the skyscrapers, astounded. In Andalusia his desires were able to finish their arc; they slipped out into the countryside and into people like notes into the wood of a cello, into olive groves on a windy day, deaf children, unmarried women at mass, fruit being eaten in the full moon, gypsies fighting with knives that flashed like fishes . . . in some way these events allowed his energy to return to him. But in New York, Lorca found not stone, but concrete. He found jagged buildings climbing like barren stairs, cowed plants, men working at jobs without possibility of grace, science insulting, men and women in the suburbs staggering around like people after a shipwreck, as if a ship had gone down in their veins. His desire-energy becomes bottled up, grows desperate, and bursts out in wild images, poems of desperate power and compassion:

> *In the graveyard far off there is a corpse*
> *who has moaned for three years*
> *because of a dry countryside in his knee;*
> *and that boy they buried this morning cried so much*
> *it was necessary to call out the dogs to keep him quiet.*

The poems do not exclude the social, even though the suffering is deeply internal, but show what is blocking the desire-energy, in others as well as in himself, with images of great precision:

> *There is a wire stretched from the Sphinx to the safety*
> *   deposit box*
> *that passes through the heart of all poor children.*

The Spanish do not know what to make of *The Poet in New York,* and some critics consider it an aberration, or say flatly that it is exaggerated, or mad. Spain being still largely unindustrialized, they do not realize that it is an understatement. I think it is a marvelous understatement, and what we need above all are clear translations of the whole book.

III

Some children in one of Lorca's early poems ask him why he is leaving the square where they all are playing, and he says, "I want to find magicians and princesses!" They ask him then, if, having come upon "the path of the poets," he will go far away from their square, and far away from the sea and the earth. He answers:

My heart of silk
is filled with lights,
with lost bells,
with lilies and bees.
I will go very far,
farther than those mountains,
farther than the oceans,
way up near the stars,
to ask the Christ the Lord
to give back to me
the soul I had as a child,
matured by fairy tales,
with its hat of feathers
and its wooden sword.

There is no other poet like him in the history of poetry. Everyone who reads a poem of Lorca's falls in love with him, and has a secret friend. All the rest of his life, whenever he thinks of Lorca, he notices a red ray of sunlight hit the ground a few inches from his feet.

from

Early Poems

Libro de Poemas *(1921)*

Poema del Cante Jondo *(1921)*

Canciones *(1924)*

PREGUNTAS

Un pleno de cigarras tiene el campo.
—¿Qué dices, Marco Aurelio,
de estas viejas filósofas del llano?
¡Pobre es tu pensamiento!

Corre el agua del río mansamente.
—¡Oh Sócrates! ¿Qué ves
en el agua que va a la amarga muerte?
¡Pobre y triste es tu fe!

Se deshojan las rosas en el lodo.
—¡Oh dulce Juan de Dios!
¿Qué ves en estos pétalos gloriosos?
¡Chico es tu corazón!

QUESTIONS

A parliament of grasshoppers is in the field.
What do you say, Marcus Aurelius,
about these old philosophers of the prairie?
Your thought is so full of poverty!

The waters of the river move slowly.
Oh Socrates! What do you see
in the water moving toward its bitter death?
Your faith is full of poverty and sad!

The leaves of the roses fall in the mud.
Oh sweet John of God!
What do you see in these magnificent petals?
Your heart is tiny!

EL NINO MUDO

El niño busca su voz.
(La tenía el rey de los grillos.)
En una gota de agua
buscaba su voz el niño.

No la quiero para hablar;
me haré con ella un anillo
que llevará mi silencio
en su dedo pequeñito.

En una gota de agua
buscaba su voz el niño.

(La voz cautiva, a lo lejos,
se ponía un traje de grillo.)

THE BOY UNABLE TO SPEAK

The small boy is looking for his voice.
(The King of the Crickets had it.)
The boy was looking
in a drop of water for his voice.

I don't want the voice to speak with;
I will make a ring from it
that my silence will wear
on its little finger.

The small boy was looking
in a drop of water for his voice.

(Far away the captured voice
was getting dressed up like a cricket.)

En el blanco infinito,
nieve, nardo y salina,
perdió su fantasía.

El color blanco, anda,
sobre una muda alfombra
de plumas de paloma.

Sin ojos ni ademán
inmóvil sufre un sueño.
Pero tiembla por dentro.

En el blanco infinito,
¡qué pura y larga herida
dejó su fantasía!

En el blanco infinito.
Nieve. Nardo. Salina.

JUAN RAMON JIMENEZ

Into the infinite white,
snow, spice-plants, and salt he took
his imagination, and left it.

The color white is walking
over a silent carpet
made of the feathers of a dove.

With no eyes or gestures
it takes in a dream without moving.
But it trembles inside.

In the infinite white
his imagination left
such a pure and deep wound!

In the infinite white.
Snow. Spice-plants. Salt.

MALAGUENA

La muerte
entra y sale
de la taberna.

Pasan caballos negros
y gente siniestra
por los hondos caminos
de la guitarra.

Y hay un olor a sal
y a sangre de hembra,
en los nardos febriles
de la marina.

La muerte
entra y sale,
y sale y entra
la muerte
de la taberna.

MALAGUENA

Death
is coming in and leaving
the tavern.

Black horses and sinister
people are riding
over the deep roads
of the guitar.

There is an odor of salt
and the blood of women
in the feverish spice-plants
by the sea.

Death
is coming in and leaving
the tavern,
death
leaving and coming in.

CANCION DE JINETE

Córdoba.
Lejana y sola.

Jaca negra, luna grande,
y aceitunas en mi alforja.
Aunque sepa los caminos
yo nunca llegaré a Córdoba.

Por el llano, por el viento,
jaca negra, luna roja.
La muerte me está mirando
desde las torres de Córdoba.

¡Ay qué camino tan largo!
¡Ay mi jaca valerosa!
¡Ay que la muerte me espera,
antes de llegar a Córdoba!

Córdoba.
Lejana y sola.

SONG OF THE RIDER

Córdoba.
Distant and alone.

Black pony, full moon,
and olives inside my saddlebag.
Though I know the roads well,
I will never arrive at Córdoba.

Over the low plains, over the winds,
black pony, red moon.
Death is looking down at me
from the towers of Córdoba.

What a long road this is!
What a brave horse I have!
Death is looking for me
before I get to Córdoba!

Córdoba.
Distant and alone.

LA GUITARRA

Empieza el llanto
de la guitarra.
Se rompen las copas
de la madrugada.
Empieza el llanto
de la guitarra.
Es inútil callarla.
Es imposible
callarla.
Llora monótona
como llora el agua,
como llora el viento
sobre la nevada.
Es imposible
callarla.
Llora por cosas
lejanas.
Arena del Sur caliente
que pide camelias blancas.
Llora flecha sin blanco,
la tarde sin mañana,
y el primer pájaro muerto
sobre la rama.
¡Oh guitarra!
Corazón malherido
por cinco espadas.

THE GUITAR

The crying of the guitar
starts.
The goblets
of the dawn break.
The crying of the guitar
starts.
No use to stop it.
It is impossible
to stop it.
It cries repeating itself
as the water cries,
as the wind cries
over the snow.
It is impossible
to stop it.
It is crying for things
far off.
The warm sand of the South
that asks for white camellias.
For the arrow with nothing to hit,
the evening with no dawn coming,
and the first bird of all dead
on the branch.
Guitar!
Heart wounded, gravely,
by five swords.

LA SOLTERA EN MISA

Bajo el Moisés del incienso,
adormecida.

Ojos de toro te miraban.
Tu rosario llovía.

Con ese traje de profunda seda,
no te muevas, Virginia.

Da los negros melones de tus pechos
al rumor de la misa.

THE UNMARRIED WOMAN AT MASS

Beneath the Moses of the incense,
asleep.

Eyes of bulls were looking at you.
Your rosary was raining.

In that dress of deep silk,
do not move, Virginia.

Give the black melons of your breasts
to the whispers of the mass.

LA LUNA ASOMA

Cuando sale la luna
se pierden las campanas
y aparecen las sendas
impenetrables.

Cuando sale la luna,
el mar cubre la tierra
y el corazón se siente
isla en el infinito.

Nadie come naranjas
bajo la luna llena.
Es preciso comer
fruta verde y helada.

Cuando sale la luna
de cien rostros iguales,
la moneda de plata
solloza en el bolsillo.

THE MOON SAILS OUT

When the moon sails out
the church bells die away
and the paths overgrown
with brush appear.

When the moon sails out
the waters cover the earth
and the heart feels it is
a little island in the infinite.

No one eats oranges
under the full moon.
The right things are fruits
green and chilled.

When the moon sails out
with a hundred faces all the same,
the coins made of silver
break out in sobs in the pocket.

from

Romancero Gitano

1927

REYERTA

A Rafael Méndez

En la mitad del barranco
las navajas de Albacete,
bellas de sangre contraria,
relucen como los peces.
Una dura luz de naipe
recorta en el agrio verde,
caballos enfurecidos
y perfiles de jinetes.
En la copa de un olivo
lloran dos viejas mujeres.
El toro de la reyerta
se sube por las paredes.
Angeles negros traían
pañuelos y agua de nieve.
Angeles con grandes alas
de navajas de Albacete.
Juan Antonio el de Montilla
rueda muerto la pendiente,
su cuerpo lleno de lirios
y una granada en las sienes.
Ahora monta cruz de fuego,
carretera de la muerte.

❀

El juez, con guardia civil,
por los olivares viene.

THE QUARREL

For Rafael Méndez

The Albacete knives, magnificent
with stranger-blood,
flash like fishes
on the gully slope.
Light crisp as a playing
card snips out of bitter
green the profiles of riders
and maddened horses.
Two old women in an olive
tree are sobbing.
The bull of the quarrel
is rising up the walls.
Black angels arrived
with handkerchiefs and snow water.
Angels with immense wings
like Albacete knives.
Juan Antonio from Montilla
rolls dead down the hill,
his body covered with lilies,
a pomegranate on his temples.
He is riding now on the cross of fire,
on the highway of death.

✿

The State Police and the judge
come along through the olive grove.

Sangre resbalada gime
muda canción de serpiente.
"Señores guardias civiles:
aquí pasó lo de siempre.
Han muerto cuatro romanos
y cinco cartagineses."

❋

La tarde loca de higueras
y de rumores calientes
cae desmayada en los muslos
heridos de los jinetes.
Y ángeles negros volaban
por el aire de poniente.
Angeles de largas trenzas
y corazones de aceite.

From the earth loosed blood moans
the silent folksong of the snake.
"Well, your honor, you see,
it's the same old business—
four Romans are dead
and five Carthaginians."

*

Dusk that the fig trees and the
hot whispers have made hysterical
faints and falls on the bloody
thighs of the riders,
and black angels went on flying
through the failing light,
angels with long hair,
and hearts of olive-oil.

THAMAR Y AMNON

Para Alfonso García-Valdecasas

La luna gira en el cielo
sobre las tierras sin agua
mientras el verano siembra
rumores de tigre y llama.
Por encima de los techos
nervios de metal sonaban.
Aire rizado venía
con los balidos de lana.
La tierra se ofrece llena
de heridas cicatrizadas,
o estremecida de agudos
cauterios de luces blancas.

❋

Thamar estaba soñando
pájaros en su garganta,
al son de panderos fríos
y cítaras enlunadas.
Su desnudo en el alero,
agudo norte de palma,
pide copos a su vientre
y granizo a sus espaldas.
Thamar estaba cantando
desnuda por la terraza.

❋

Alrededor de sus pies,
cinco palomas heladas.

THAMAR AND AMNON

For Alfonso García-Valdecasas

The moon turns in the sky
above the dry fields
and the summer plants
rumors of tiger and flame.
Nerves of metal
resonated over the roofs.
Bleatings made of wool
arrived on curly winds.
The earth lies covered
with scarred-over wounds,
or shaken by the sharp
burnings of white stars.

❁

Thamar was dreaming of
birds in her throat.
She heard frosty tambourines
and moon-covered zithers.
Her nakedness on the roof,
a palm pointing north,
asks for snowflakes at her stomach,
and hailstones at her shoulders.
Thamar was there singing
naked on the roof-top.

∗

Huddled near her feet
five frozen doves.

Amnón, delgado y concreto,
en la torre la miraba,
llenas las ingles de espuma
y oscilaciones la barba.
Su desnudo iluminado
se tendía en la terraza,
con un rumor entre dientes
de flecha recién clavada.
Amnón estaba mirando
la luna redonda y baja,
y vió en la luna los pechos
durísimos de su hermana.

*

Amnón a las tres y media
se tendió sobre la cama.
Toda la alcoba sufría
con sus ojos llenos de alas.
La luz, maciza, sepulta
pueblos en la arena parda,
o descubre transitorio
coral de rosas y dalias.
Linfa de pozo oprimida
brota silencio en las jarras.
En el musgo de los troncos
la cobra tendida canta.
Amnón gime por la tela
fresquísima de la cama.
Yedra del escalofrío
cubre su carne quemada.
Thamar entró silenciosa

Amnon, lithe and firm,
watched her from his tower.
His genitals were like surf,
and his beard swaying.
Her luminous nakedness
stretched out on the terrace,
her teeth sound like an arrow
that has just hit its mark.
Amnon was looking over
at the round and heavy moon,
and he saw there the hard
breasts of his sister.

❀

At three-thirty Amnon
threw himself on his bed.
The hundred wings in his eyes
disturbed the whole room.
The moonlight, massive, buries
towns under dark sand,
or opens a mortal coral
of dahlias and roses.
Underground water oppressed
breaks its silence in jars.
The cobra is singing on the tree,
stretched out on the mosses.
Amnon groans from the fresh
sheets of his bed.
An ivy of icy fever
covers his burning body.
Thamar walked silently

131

en la alcoba silenciada,
color de vena y Danubio,
turbia de huellas lejanas.
—Thamar, bórrame los ojos
con tu fija madrugada.
Mis hilos de sangre tejen
volantes sobre tu falda.
—Déjame tranquila, hermano.
Son tus besos en mi espalda
avispas y vientecillos
en doble enjambre de flautas.
—Thamar, en tus pechos altos
hay dos peces que me llaman,
y en las yemas de tus dedos
rumor de rosa encerrada.

❊

Los cien caballos del rey
en el patio relinchaban.
Sol en cubos resistía
la delgadez de la parra.
Ya la coge del cabello,
ya la camisa le rasga.
Corales tibios dibujan
arroyos en rubio mapa.

❊

¡Oh, qué gritos se sentían
por encima de las casas!
Qué espesura de puñales
y túnicas desgarradas.

into the silence of his bedroom,
the color of blood and Danube
troubled with far off footprints.
"Thamar, put out my eyes
with your piercing dawn.
The threads of my blood
are weaving the folds on your dress."
"Leave me be, brother.
Your kisses are wasps
on my shoulder, and winds blowing
in a double twirling of flutes."
"Thamar, I hear two fishes
calling me from your steep breasts,
and the sound of closed rosebuds
in the tips of your fingers."

❋

The hundred horses of the king
neigh together in the courtyard.
The sun in buckets fought
the slenderness of the vine.
Now he takes her by the hair,
now he rips her dress.
Warm corals start drawing
rivulets on a blond country.

❋

What screams are heard now
lifting above the houses!
What a thicket of knives,
and cloaks torn up!

133

Por las escaleras tristes
esclavos suben y bajan.
Embolos y muslos juegan
bajo las nubes paradas.
Alrededor de Thamar
gritan vírgenes gitanas
y otras recogen las gotas
de su flor martirizada.
Paños blancos enrojecen
en las alcobas cerradas.
Rumores de tibia aurora
pámpanos y peces cambian.

❋

Violador enfurecido,
Amnón huye con su jaca.
Negros le dirigen flechas
en los muros y atalayas.
Y cuando los cuatro cascos
eran cuatro resonancias,
David con unas tijeras
cortó las cuerdas del arpa.

Slaves keep going up
the sad stairs and back down.
Pistons and thighs play
under the motionless clouds.
Standing around Thamar
gypsy virgins give cries,
others gather up the drops
of her murdered flower.
White fabrics slowly turn red
in the locked bedrooms.
At first whisper of warm dawn
fish turn back into tendrils.

*

The raper, Amnon, flees,
wild, on his horse.
Negroes shoot arrows
at him from the parapets.
When the beat of the four hoofs
became four fading chords,
David took a scissors
and cut the strings of his harp.

135

PRECIOSA Y EL AIRE

A Dámaso Alonso

Su luna de pergamino
Preciosa tocando viene
por un anfibio sendero
de cristales y laureles.
El silencio sin estrellas,
huyendo del sonsonete,
cae donde el mar bate y canta
su noche llena de peces.
En los picos de la sierra
los carabineros duermen
guardando las blancas torres
donde viven los ingleses.
Y los gitanos del agua
levantan por distraerse,
glorietas de caracolas
y ramas de pino verde.

＊

Su luna de pergamino
Preciosa tocando viene.
Al verla se ha levantado
el viento que nunca duerme.
San Cristobalón desnudo,
lleno de lenguas celestes,
mira a la niña tocando
una dulce gaita ausente.

＊

—Niña, deja que levante

PRECIOSA AND THE WIND

for Dámaso Alonso

Preciosa comes along,
playing her parchment moon,
down an amphibious path
of laurel trees and water lights.
The silence without stars
fleeing from all this noise
falls over where the high seas sing
about their fish-filled night.
The sentries on the mountain
peaks are asleep,
keeping watch over the white
towers where the English live.
And the river gypsies
to pass the time build summer
houses out of seashells
and evergreen boughs.

❋

Preciosa strolls along,
picking her parchment moon.
Seeing her, the wind
who never sleeps rises,
and St. Christopher, huge and naked,
a storehouse of divine tongues,
watches the girl playing
on some soft and absent pipes.

❋

"Sweetheart, let me lift up

tu vestido para verte.
Abre en mis dedos antiguos
la rosa azul de tu vientre.

Preciosa tira el pandero
y corre sin detenerse.
El viento-hombrón la persigue
con una espada caliente.

Frunce su rumor el mar.
Los olivos palidecen.
Cantan las flautas de umbría
y el liso gong de la nieve.

¡Preciosa, corre, Preciosa,
que te coge el viento verde!
¡Preciosa, corre, Preciosa!
¡Míralo por donde viene!
Sátiro de estrellas bajas
con sus lenguas relucientes.

❂

Preciosa, llena de miedo,
entra en la casa que tiene,
más arriba de los pinos,
el cónsul de los ingleses.

Asustados por los gritos
tres carabineros vienen,
sus negras capas ceñidas
y los gorros en las sienes.

your dress and have a look.
Open the blue rose
of your belly for my old fingers."

  Preciosa tosses the tambourine
  and runs wildly.
The horny wind runs after
with a hot sword.

  The sea puckers up its sound.
The olives turn pale.
The flutes of darkness call,
and the sleek gong of the snow.

  Run, Preciosa, run!
The green wind will get you!
Run, Preciosa, run!
Look, he's gaining on you!
Goat-man of deep-voiced stars
with luminous tongues.

❀

  Terrified, Preciosa
runs into the villa
—high above the pine trees—
where the English consul lives.

  Three sentries frightened
by her cries come down,
their black capes buckled,
caps pulled too far down.

139

El inglés da a la gitana
un vaso de tibia leche,
y una copa de ginebra
que Preciosa no se bebe.

Y mientras cuenta, llorando,
su aventura a aquella gente,
en las tejas de pizarra
el viento, furioso, muerde.

The Englishman gives a tumbler
of warm milk to the gypsy,
and a shotglass of gin,
which Preciosa refuses.

All the time she's telling
—crying—her adventure,
the wind, enraged, bites
the tiles on the roof.

from

Poeta en Nueva York

1930

VUELTA DE PASEO

Asesinado por el cielo,
entre las formas que van hacia la sierpe
y las formas que buscan el cristal,
dejaré crecer mis cabellos.

Con el árbol de muñones que no canta
y el niño con el blanco rostro de huevo.

Con los animalitos de cabeza rota
y el agua harapienta de los pies secos.

Con todo lo que tiene cansancio sordomudo
y mariposa ahogada en el tintero.

Tropezando con mi rostro distinto de cada día.
¡Asesinado por el cielo!

HOME FROM A WALK

Assassinated by the sky,
between the forms that are moving toward the serpent,
and the forms that are moving toward the crystal,
I'll let my hair fall down.

With the tree of amputated limbs that does not sing,
and the boy with the white face of an egg.

With all the tiny animals who have broken heads,
and the ragged water that walks on its dry feet.

With all the things that have a deaf and dumb fatigue,
and the butterfly drowned in the inkpot.

Stumbling over my face that changes every day,
assassinated by the sky!

IGLESIA ABANDONADA

(Balada de la Gran Guerra)

Yo tenía un hijo que se llamaba Juan.
Yo tenía un hijo.
Se perdió por los arcos un viernes de todos los muertos.
Le ví jugar en las últimas escaleras de la misa
y echaba un cubito de hojalata en el corazón del sacerdote.
He golpeado los ataúdes. ¡Mi hijo! ¡Mi hijo! ¡Mi hijo!
Saqué una pata de gallina por detrás de la luna y luego,
comprendí que mi niña era un pez
por donde se alejan las carretas.
Yo tenía una niña.
Yo tenía un pez muerto bajo la ceniza de los incensarios.
Yo tenía un mar. ¿De qué? ¡Dios mío! ¡Un mar!
Subí a tocar las campanas, pero las frutas tenían gusanos
y las cerillas apagadas
se comían los trigos de la primavera.
Yo ví la transparente cigüeña de alcohol
mondar las negras cabezas de los soldados agonizantes
y ví las cabañas de goma
donde giraban las copas llenas de lágrimas.
En las anémonas del ofertorio te encontraré, ¡corazón mío!
cuando el sacerdote levante la mula y el buey con sus fuertes
      brazos
para espantar los sapos nocturnos que rondan los helados
      paisajes del cáliz.
Yo tenía un hijo que era un gigante,
pero los muertos son más fuertes y saben devorar pedazos de
      cielo.

RUNDOWN CHURCH

(Ballad of the First World War)

I had a son and his name was John.
I had a son.
He disappeared into the arches one Friday of All Souls.
I saw him playing on the highest steps of the Mass
throwing a little tin pail at the heart of the priest.
I knocked on the coffin. My son! My son! My son!
I drew out a chicken foot from behind the moon and then
I understood that my daughter was a fish
down which the carts vanish.
I had a daughter.
I had a fish dead under the ashes of the incense burner.
I had an ocean. Of what? Good Lord! An ocean!
I went up to ring the bells but the fruit was all wormy
and the blackened match-ends
were eating the spring wheat.
I saw a stork of alcohol you could see through
shaving the black heads of the dying soldiers
and I saw the rubber booths
where the goblets full of tears were whirling.
In the anemones of the offertory I will find you, my love!
when the priest with his strong arms raises up the mule and
    the ox
to scare the nighttime toads that roam in the icy landscapes of
    the chalice.
I had a son who was a giant,
but the dead are stronger and know how to gobble down pieces
    of the sky.

147

Si mi niño hubiera sido un oso,
yo no temería el sigilo de los caimanes,
ni hubiese visto el mar amarrado a los árboles
para ser fornicado y herido por el tropel de los regimientos.
¡Si mi niño hubiera sido un oso!
Me envolveré sobre esta lona dura para no sentir el frío de los
    musgos.
Sé muy bien que me darán una manga o la corbata;
pero en el centro de la misa yo romperé el timón y entonces
vendrá a la piedra la locura de pingüinos y gaviotas
que harán decir a los que duermen y a los que cantan por las
    esquinas:
él tenía un hijo.
¡Un hijo! ¡Un hijo! ¡Un hijo
que no era más que suyo, porque era su hijo!
¡Su hijo! ¡Su hijo! ¡Su hijo!

If my son had only been a bear,
I wouldn't fear the secrecy of the crocodiles
and I wouldn't have seen the ocean roped to the trees
to be raped and wounded by the mobs from the regiment.
If my son had only been a bear!
I'll roll myself in this rough canvas so as not to feel the chill of
    the mosses.
I know very well they will give me a sleeve or a necktie,
but in the innermost part of the Mass I'll smash the rudder and
then
the insanity of the penguins and seagulls will come to the
rock
and they will make the people sleeping and the people singing
    on the streetcorners say:
he had a son.
A son! A son! A son
and it was no one else's, because it was his son!
His son! His son! His son!

DANZA DE LA MUERTE

El mascarón. ¡Mirad el mascarón!
¡Cómo viene del África a New York!

Se fueron los árboles de la pimienta,
los pequeños botones de fósforo.
Se fueron los camellos de carne desgarrada
y los valles de luz que el cisne levantaba con el pico.

Era el momento de las cosas secas,
de la espiga en el ojo y el gato laminado,
del óxido de hierro de los grandes puentes
y el definitivo silencio del corcho.

Era la gran reunión de los animales muertos,
traspasados por las espadas de la luz;
la alegría eterna del hipopótamo con las pezuñas de ceniza
y de la gacela con una siempreviva en la garganta.

En la marchita soledad sin onda
el abollado mascarón danzaba.
Medio lado del mundo era de arena,
mercurio y sol dormido el otro medio.

El mascarón. ¡Mirad el mascarón!
¡Arena, caimán y miedo sobre Nueva York!

*

Desfiladeros de cal aprisionaban un cielo vacío
donde sonaban las voces de los que mueren bajo el guano.
Un cielo mondado y puro, idéntico a sí mismo,
con el bozo y lirio agudo de sus montañas invisibles,

DANCE OF DEATH

The mask. Look at the mask!
It's coming from Africa to New York!

The pepper trees are all gone,
the tiny buds of phosphorus with them.
The camels made of torn flesh are gone
and the valleys of light the swan carried in his bill.

It was the time of dried things,
of the wheat-beard in the eye, and the flattened cat,
of rusting iron on the giant bridges
and the absolute silence of cork.

It was the grand reunion of the dead animals,
cut through by blades of light;
the eternal joy of the hippopotamus with his hoofs of ash,
and the gazelle with an everlasting in its throat.

In the withered solitude without waves,
the dented mask was dancing.
One half of the world was made of sand,
the other half was mercury and the sun asleep.

The black mask. Look at the mask!
Sand, crocodile, and fear over New York!

*

Mountain passes of lime were walling in the empty sky;
you heard the voices of those dying under the dung of birds.
A sky, clipped and pure, exactly like itself,
with the fluff and sharp-edged lily of its invisible mountains,

acabó con los más leves tallitos del canto
y se fue al diluvio empaquetado de la savia,
a través del descanso de los últimos desfiles,
levantando con el rabo pedazos de espejo.

Cuando el chino lloraba en el tejado
sin encontrar el desnudo de su mujer
y el director del banco observando el manómetro
que mide el cruel silencio de la moneda,
el mascarón llegaba al Wall Street.

No es extraño para la danza
este columbario que pone los ojos amarillos.
De la esfinge a la caja de caudales hay un hilo tenso
que atraviesa el corazón de todos los niños pobres.
El ímpetu primitivo baila con el ímpetu mecánico,
ignorantes en su frenesí de la luz original.
Porque si la rueda olvida su fórmula,
ya puede cantar desnuda con las manadas de caballos:
y si una llama quema los helados proyectos,
el cielo tendrá que huir ante el tumulto de las ventanas.

No es extraño este sitio para la danza, yo lo digo.
El mascarón bailará entre columnas de sangre y de números,
entre huracanes de oro y gemidos de obreros parados
que aullarán, noche oscura, por tu tiempo sin luces,
¡oh salvaje Norteamérica!, ¡oh impúdica!, ¡oh salvaje,
tendida en la frontera de la nieve!

has killed the most delicate stems of song,
and gone off to the flood crowded with sap,
across the resting time of the final marchers,
lifting bits of mirror with its tail.

While the Chinaman was crying on the roof
without finding the nakedness of his wife,
and the bank president was watching the pressure-gauge
that measures the remorseless silence of money,
the black mask was arriving at Wall Street.

This vault that makes the eyes turn yellow
is not an odd place for dancing.
There is a wire stretched from the Sphinx to the safety
    deposit box
that passes through the heart of all poor children.
The primitive energy is dancing with the machine energy,
in their frenzy wholly ignorant of the original light.
Because if the wheel forgets its formula,
it might as well sing naked with the herds of horses;
and if a flame burns up the frozen plans
the sky will have to run away from the roar of the windows.

This place is a good place for dancing, I say this truth,
the black mask will dance between columns of blood and
    numbers,
between downpours of gold and groans of unemployed workers
who will go howling, dark night, through your time without
    stars.
O savage North America! shameless! savage,
stretched out on the frontier of the snow!

El mascarón. ¡Mirad el mascarón!
¡Qué ola de fango y luciérnaga sobre Nueva York!

*

Yo estaba en la terraza luchando con la luna.
Enjambres de ventanas acribillaban un muslo de la noche.
En mis ojos bebían las dulces vacas de los cielos.
Y las brisas de largos remos
golpeaban los cenicientos cristales de Broadway.

La gota de sangre buscaba la luz de la yema del astro
para fingir una muerta semilla de manzana.
El aire de la llanura, empujado por los pastores,
temblaba con un miedo de molusco sin concha.

Pero no son los muertos los que bailan,
estoy seguro.
Los muertos están embebidos, devorando sus propias manos.
Son los otros los que bailan con el mascarón y su vihuela;
son los otros, los borrachos de plata, los hombres fríos,
los que crecen en el cruce de los muslos y llamas duras,
los que buscan la lombriz en el paisaje de las escaleras,
los que beben en el banco de lágrimas de niña muerta
o los que comen por las esquinas diminutas pirámides del alba.

¡Que no baile el Papa!
¡No, que no baile el Papa!
Ni el Rey,
ni el millonario de dientes azules,
ni las bailarinas secas de las catedrales,

The black mask! Look at the black mask!
What a wave of filth and glow worms over New York!

✿

I was out on the terrace fighting with the moon.
Swarms of windows were stinging one of the night's thighs.
The gentle sky-cows were drinking from my eyes.
And winds with immense oars
were beating on the ash-colored lights of Broadway.

A drop of blood was looking for the light at the yolk of
    the star
in order to imitate the dead seed of an apple.
A wind from the prairies, pushed along by the shepherds,
shivered with the fear of a mollusc with no shell.

But the dead are not the ones dancing,
I'm sure of that.
The dead are totally absorbed, gobbling up their own hands.
It's the others who have to dance with the black mask and its
    guitar;
it's the others, men drunk on silver, the frosty men,
those who thrive at the crossroads of thighs and mineral fires,
those who are searching for the worm in the landscape of
    staircases,
those who drink the tears of a dead girl in a bank vault,
or those who eat in the corners the tiny pyramids of the dawn.

I don't want the Pope to dance!
No, I don't want the Pope to dance!
Nor the King,
nor the millionaire with his blue teeth,
nor the withered dancers of the cathedrals,

ni constructores, ni esmeraldas, ni locos, ni sodomitas.
Sólo este mascarón,
este mascarón de vieja escarlatina,
¡sólo este mascarón!

Que ya las cobras silbarán por los últimos pisos,
que ya las ortigas estremecerán patios y terrazas,
que ya la Bolsa será una pirámide de musgo,
que ya vendrán lianas después de los fusiles
y muy pronto, muy pronto, muy pronto.
¡Ay, Wall Street!

El mascarón. ¡Mirad el mascarón!
¡Cómo escupe veneno de bosque
por la angustia imperfecta de Nueva York!

Diciembre 1929

nor the carpenters, nor emeralds, nor madmen, nor corn-holers.
I want this mask to dance,
this mask with its musty scarlet,
just this mask!

Because now the cobras will whistle on the highest floors,
and the stinging weeds will make the patios and terraces
    tremble,
because the stock market will be a pyramid of moss,
because the jungle creepers will come after the rifles
and soon, soon, very soon!
Look out, Wall Street!

The mask, the mask. Look at the mask!
How it spits the poison of the forest
over the faulty pain of New York!

December 1929

CIUDAD SIN SUENO

(Nocturno del Brooklyn Bridge)

No duerme nadie por el cielo. Nadie, nadie.
No duerme nadie.
Las criaturas de la luna huelen y rondan sus cabañas.
Vendrán las iguanas vivas a morder a los hombres que no
    sueñan
y el que huye con el corazón roto encontrará por las esquinas
al increíble cocodrilo quieto bajo la tierna protesta de los
    astros.

No duerme nadie por el mundo. Nadie, nadie.
No duerme nadie.
Hay un muerto en el cementerio más lejano
que se queja tres años
porque tiene un paisaje seco en la rodilla;
y el niño que enterraron esta mañana lloraba tanto
que hubo necesidad de llamar a los perros para que callase.

No es sueño la vida. ¡Alerta! ¡Alerta! ¡Alerta!
Nos caemos por las escaleras para comer la tierra húmeda
o subimos al filo de la nieve con el coro de las dalias muertas.
Pero no hay olvido, ni sueño:
carne viva. Los besos atan las bocas
en una maraña de venas recientes
y al que le duele su dolor le dolerá sin descanso
y al que teme la muerte la llevará sobre sus hombros.

Un día
las caballos vivirán en las tabernas

CITY THAT DOES NOT SLEEP

(Nightsong of Brooklyn Bridge)

In the sky there is nobody asleep. Nobody, nobody.
Nobody is asleep.
The creatures of the moon sniff and prowl about their cabins.
The living iguanas will come to bite the men who do not dream,
and the man who rushes out with his spirit broken will meet on
    the streetcorner
the unbelievable alligator quiet beneath the tender protest of
    the stars.

Nobody is asleep on earth. Nobody, nobody.
Nobody is asleep.
In the graveyard far off there is a corpse
who has moaned for three years
because of a dry countryside in his knee;
and that boy they buried this morning cried so much
it was necessary to call out the dogs to keep him quiet.

Life is not a dream. Careful! Careful! Careful!
We fall down the stairs in order to eat the moist earth
or we climb to the knife-edge of the snow with the voices of
    the dead dahlias.
But forgetfulness does not exist, dreams do not exist;
flesh exists. Kisses tie our mouths
in a thicket of new veins,
and whoever his pain pains will feel that pain forever
and whoever is afraid of death will carry it on his shoulders.

One day
the horses will live in the saloons

y las hormigas furiosas
atacarán los cielos amarillos que se refugian en los ojos de
    las vacas.
    Otro día
veremos la resurrección de las mariposas disecadas
y aún andando por un paisaje de esponjas grises y barcos mudos
veremos brillar nuestro anillo y manar rosas de nuestra lengua.

¡Alerta! ¡Alerta! ¡Alerta!
A los que guardan todavía huellas de zarpa y aguacero,
a aquel muchacho que llora porque no sabe la invención del
    puente
o a aquel muerto que ya no tiene más que la cabeza y un zapato,
hay que llevarlos al muro donde iguanas y sierpes esperan,
donde espera la dentadura del oso,
donde espera la mano momificada del niño
y la piel del camello se eriza con un violento escalofrío azul.

    No duerme nadie por el cielo. Nadie, nadie.
No duerme nadie.
Pero si alguien cierra los ojos,
¡azotadlo, hijos míos, azotadlo!
Haya un panorama de ojos abiertos
y amargas llagas encendidas.
No duerme nadie por el mundo. Nadie, nadie.
Ya lo he dicho.
No duerme nadie.
Pero si alguien tiene por la noche exceso de musgo en las sienes,
abrid los escotillones para que vea bajo la luna
las copas falsas, el veneno y la calavera de los teatros.

and the enraged ants
will throw themselves on the yellow skies that take refuge in the
     eyes of cows.
   Another day
we will watch the preserved butterflies rise from the dead
and still walking through a country of gray sponges and silent
     boats
we will watch our ring flash and roses spring from our tongue.
Careful! Be careful! Be careful!
The men who still have marks of the claw and the thunderstorm,
and that boy who cries because he has never heard of the
     invention of the bridge,
or that dead man who only possesses now his head and a shoe,
we must carry them to the wall where the iguanas and the snakes
     are waiting,
where the bear's teeth are waiting,
where the mummified hand of the boy is waiting,
and the hair of the camel stands on end with a violent blue
     shudder.

   Nobody is sleeping in the sky. Nobody, nobody.
Nobody is sleeping.
If someone does close his eyes,
a whip, boys, a whip!
Let there be a landscape of open eyes
and bitter wounds on fire.
No one is sleeping in this world. No one, no one.
I have said it before.
No one is sleeping.
But if someone grows too much moss on his temples during the
     night,
open the stage trapdoors so he can see in the moonlight
the lying goblets, and the poison, and the skull of the theaters.

LA AURORA

La aurora de Nueva York tiene
cuatro columnas de cieno
y un huracán de negras palomas
que chapotean las aguas podridas.

La aurora de Nueva York gime
por las inmensas escaleras
buscando entre las aristas
nardos de angustia dibujada.

La aurora llega y nadie la recibe en su boca
porque allí no hay mañana ni esperanza posible.
A veces las monedas en enjambres furiosos
taladran y devoran abandonados niños.

Los primeros que salen comprenden con sus huesos
que no habrá paraíso ni amores deshojados;
saben que van al cieno de números y leyes,
a los juegos sin arte, a sudores sin fruto.

La luz es sepultada por cadenas y ruidos
en impúdico reto de ciencia sin raíces.
Por los barrios hay gentes que vacilan insomnes
como recién salidas de un naufragio de sangre.

SUNRISE

The sunrise of New York
has four columns of filth
and a hurricane of black pigeons
that putter in the putrid waters.

The sunrise of New York groans
up the immense staircases
searching along the sharp edges
for etched spice-plants of anguish.

The sunrise arrives, and no one opens his mouth to receive it,
because neither tomorrow nor hope is possible here.
Only now and then mad swarms of nickels and dimes
sting and eat the abandoned children.

The first to leave their houses know in their bones
there'll be no paradise and no love without leaves;
they know they are going to the filth of numbers and laws,
to the games anyone can play, and the work without fruit.

The light is already buried by chains and noises
in the ugly threat of science that has no roots.
Through the suburbs people who cannot sleep are staggering
as though recently rescued from a shipwreck of blood.

MUERTE

Para Rafael Sánchez Ventura

¡Qué esfuerzo!
¡Qué esfuerzo del caballo por ser perro!
¡Qué esfuerzo del perro por ser golondrina!
¡Qué esfuerzo de la golondrina por ser abeja!
¡Qué esfuerzo de la abeja por ser caballo!
Y el caballo,
¡qué flecha aguda exprime de la rosa!,
¡qué rosa gris levanta de su belfo!
Y la rosa,
¡qué rebaño de luces y alaridos
ata en el vivo azúcar de su tronco!
Y el azúcar,
¡qué puñalitos sueña en su vigilia!;
y los puñales diminutos
¡qué luna sin establos, qué desnudos,
piel eterna y rubor, andan buscando!
Y yo, por los aleros,
¡qué serafín de llamas busco y soy!
Pero el arco de yeso,
¡qué grande, qué invisible, qué diminuto!,
sin esfuerzo.

DEATH

For Rafael Sánchez Ventura

So much effort!
Effort the horse makes to be a dog!
Effort the dog makes to be a swallow!
Effort the swallow makes to be a bee!
Effort the bee makes to be a horse!
And the horse,
what a sharp arrow it presses out of the rose!
What a gray rose it lifts up from its teeth!
And the rose,
what a mob of lights and barks
it ties into the living sugar of its treetrunk!
As for the sugar,
what tiny daggers it dreams of while awake!
And the tiny daggers,
what a moon without mangers, what naked bodies—
with skin eternal and blushing—they look and look for!
And I, when I am on the roof,
what a pure seraphim of fire I want to be and I am!
But this plaster arch,
how immense it is, how invisible, how tiny,
no effort at all.

PAISAJE CON DOS TUMBAS Y UN PERRO ASIRIO

Amigo,
levántate para que oigas aullar
al perro asirio.
Las tres ninfas del cáncer han estado bailando,
hijo mío.
Trajeron, unas montañas de lacre rojo
y unas sábanas duras donde estaba el cáncer dormido.
El caballo tenía un ojo en el cuello
y la luna estaba en un cielo tan frío
que tuvo que desgarrarse su monte de Venus
y ahogar en sangre y ceniza los cementerios antiguos.

Amigo,
despierta, que los montes todavía no respiran
y las hierbas de mi corazón están en otro sitio.
No importa que estés lleno de agua de mar.
Yo amé mucho tiempo a un niño
que tenía una plumilla en la lengua
y vivimos cien años dentro de un cuchillo.
Despierta. Calla. Escucha. Incorpórate un poco.
En aullido
es una larga lengua morada que deja
hormigas de espanto y licor de lirios.
Ya viene hacia la roca. ¡No alargues tus raíces!
Se acerca. Gime. No solloces en sueños, amigo.

¡Amigo!
Levántate para que oigas aullar
al perro asirio.

LANDSCAPE WITH TWO GRAVES AND AN ASSYRIAN HOUND

Get up,
my friend, so you can hear the Assyrian
hound howling.
The three nymphs of cancer are already up and dancing,
my son.
They brought along mountains of red sealing-wax,
and some rough sheets that cancer slept on last night.
The neck of the horse had an eye
and the moon was up in a sky so cold
she had to rip up her own mound of Venus
and drown the ancient cemeteries in blood and ashes.

Friend,
wake up, for the hills are still not breathing,
and the grass in my heart has gone off somewhere.
It does not matter if you are full of sea-water.
I loved a child for a long time
who had a tiny feather on his tongue
and we lived a hundred years inside a knife.
Wake up. Say nothing. Listen. Sit up a little.
The howling
is a long and purple tongue leaving behind
ants of terror and lilies that make you drunk.
It's coming near your stone now. Don't stretch out your roots!
Nearer. It's moaning. Don't sob in your sleep, my friend.

My friend,
get up, so you can hear the Assyrian hound
howling.

PEQUENO POEMA INFINITO

Para Luis Cardoza y Aragón

Equivocar el camino
es llegar a la nieve
y llegar a la nieve
es pacer durante veinte siglos las hierbas de los cementerios.

Equivocar el camino
es llegar a la mujer,
la mujer que no teme la luz,
la mujer que mata dos gallos en un segundo,
la luz que no teme a los gallos
y los gallos que no saben cantar sobre la nieve.

Pero si la nieve se equivoca de corazón
puede llegar el viento Austro
y como el aire no hace caso de los gemidos
tendremos que pacer otra vez las hierbas de los cementerios.

Yo vi dos dolorosas espigas de cera
que enterraban un paisaje de volcanes
y vi dos niños locos que empujaban llorando las pupilas de un
    asesino.

LITTLE INFINITE POEM

For Luis Cardoza y Aragón

To take the wrong road
is to arrive at the snow.
is to arrive at the snow
and to arrive at the snow
is to get down on all fours for twenty centuries and eat the
    grasses of the cemeteries.

To take the wrong road
is to arrive at woman,
woman who isn't afraid of light,
woman who murders two roosters in one second,
light which isn't afraid of roosters,
and roosters who don't know how to sing on top of the snow.

But if the snow truly takes the wrong road,
then it might meet the southern wind,
and since the air cares nothing for groans,
we will have to get down on all fours again and eat the grasses
    of the cemeteries.

I saw two mournful wheatheads made of wax
burying a countryside of volcanoes;
and I saw two insane little boys who wept as they leaned on a
    murderer's eyeballs.

Pero el dos no ha sido nunca un número
porque es una angustia y su sombra,
porque es la guitarra donde el amor se desespera,
porque es la demostración de otro infinito que no es suyo
y es las murallas del muerto
y el castigo de la nueva resurrección sin finales.
Los muertos odian el número dos,
pero el número dos adormece a las mujeres
y como la mujer teme la luz
la luz tiembla delante de los gallos
y los gallos sólo saben volar sobre la nieve
tendremos que pacer sin descanso las hierbas de los cementerios.

10 de enero de 1930. New York.

But two has never been a number—
because it's only an anguish and its shadow,
it's only a guitar where love feels how hopeless it is,
it's the proof of someone else's infinity,
and the walls around a dead man,
and the scourging of a new resurrection that will never end.
Dead people hate the number two,
but the number two makes women drop off to sleep,
and since women are afraid of light,
light shudders when it has to face the roosters,
and since all roosters know is how to fly over the snow
we will have to get down on all fours and eat the grasses of
    the cemeteries forever.

January 10, 1930. New York.

NEW YORK

(Oficina y denuncia)

A Fernando Vela

Debajo de las multiplicaciones
hay una gota de sangre de pato.
Debajo de las divisiones
hay una gota de sangre de marinero;
debajo de las sumas, un río de sangre tierna.
Un río que viene cantando
por los dormitorios de los arrabales,
y es plata, cemento o brisa
en el alba mentida de New York.
Existen las montañas. Lo sé.
Y los anteojos para la sabiduría.
Lo sé. Pero yo no he venido a ver el cielo.
Yo he venido para ver la turbia sangre.
La sangre que lleva las máquinas a las cataratas
y el espíritu a la lengua de la cobra.
Todos los días se matan en New York
cuatro millones de patos,
cinco millones de cerdos,
dos mil palomas para el gusto de los agonizantes,
un millón de vacas,
un millón de corderos
y dos millones de gallos,
que dejan los cielos hechos añicos.
Más vale sollozar afilando la navaja
o asesinar a los perros en las alucinantes cacerías,
que resistir en la madrugada

NEW YORK

(Office and Attack)

To Fernando Vela

Beneath all the statistics
there is a drop of duck's blood.
Beneath all the columns
there is a drop of a sailor's blood.
Beneath all the totals, a river of warm blood;
a river that goes singing
past the bedrooms of the suburbs,
and the river is silver, cement, or wind
in the lying daybreak of New York.
The mountains exist, I know that.
And the lenses ground for wisdom,
I know that. But I have not come to see the sky.
I have come to see the stormy blood,
the blood that sweeps the machines to the waterfalls,
and the spirit on to the cobra's tongue.
Every day they kill in New York
ducks, four million,
pigs, five million,
pigeons, two thousand, for the enjoyment of dying men,
cows, one million,
lambs, one million,
roosters, two million
who turn the sky to small splinters.
You may as well sob filing a razor blade
or assassinate dogs in the hallucinated foxhunts,
as try to stop in the dawnlight

173

los interminables trenes de leche,
los interminables trenes de sangre,
y los trenes de rosas maniatadas
por los comerciantes de perfumes.
Los patos y las palomas,
y los cerdos y los corderos
ponen sus gotas de sangre
debajo de las multiplicaciones,
y los terribles alaridos de las vacas estrujadas
llenan de dolor el valle
donde el Hudson se emborracha con aceite.
Yo denuncio a toda la gente
que ignora la otra mitad,
la mitad irredimible
que levanta sus montes de cemento
donde laten los corazones
de los animalitos que se olvidan
y donde caeremos todos
en la última fiesta de los taladros.
Os escupo en la cara.
La otra mitad me escucha
devorando, orinando, volando en su pureza,
como los niños de las porterías
que llevan frágiles palitos
a los huecos donde se oxidan
las antenas de los insectos.
No es el infierno, es la calle.
No es la muerte, es la tienda de frutas.
Hay un mundo de ríos quebrados y distancias inasibles
en la patita de ese gato quebrada por el automóvil,
y yo oigo el canto de la lombriz

the endless trains carrying milk,
the endless trains carrying blood,
and the trains carrying roses in chains
for those in the field of perfume.
The ducks and the pigeons
and the hogs and the lambs
lay their drops of blood down
underneath all the statistics;
and the terrible bawling of the packed-in cattle
fills the valley with suffering
where the Hudson is getting drunk on its oil.
I attack all those persons
who know nothing of the other half,
the half who cannot be saved,
who raise their cement mountains
in which the hearts of the small
animals no one thinks of are beating,
and from which we will all fall
during the final holiday of the drills.
I spit in your face.
The other half hears me,
as they go on eating, urinating, flying in their purity
like the children of the janitors
who carry delicate sticks
to the holes where the antennas
of the insects are rusting.
This is not hell, it is a street.
This is not death, it is a fruit-stand.
There is a whole world of crushed rivers and unachievable
        distances
in the paw of a cat crushed by a car,
and I hear the song of the worm

en el corazón de muchas niñas.
Oxido, fermento, tierra estremecida.
Tierra tú mismo que nadas por los números de la
oficina.
¿Que voy a hacer? ¿Ordenar los paisajes?
¿Ordenar los amores que luego son fotografías,
que luego son pedazos de madera y bocanadas de sangre?
No, no, no, no; yo denuncio.
Yo denuncio la conjura
de estas desiertas oficinas
que no ridian las agonías,
que borron los programas de la selva,
y me ofrezco a ser comido por las vacas estrujadas
cuando sus gritos llenan el valle
donde el Hudson se emborracha con aceite.

in the heart of so many girls.
Rust, rotting, trembling earth.
And you are earth, swimming through the figures of the office.
What shall I do, set my landscapes in order?
Set in place the lovers who will afterwards be photographs,
who will be bits of wood and mouthfuls of blood?
No, I won't; I attack,
I attack the conspiring
of these empty offices
that will not broadcast the sufferings,
that rub out the plans of the forest,
and I offer myself to be eaten by the packed-up cattle
when their mooing fills the valley
where the Hudson is getting drunk on its oil.

SON DE NEGROS EN CUBA

Cuando llegue la luna llena
iré a Santiago de Cuba.
Iré a Santiago
en un coche de agua negra.
Iré a Santiago.
Cantarán los techos de palmera.
Iré a Santiago.
Cuando la palma quiere ser cigüeña,
iré a Santiago.
Y cuando quiere ser medusa el plátano,
iré a Santiago.
Con la rubia cabeza de Fonseca.
Iré a Santiago.
Y con la rosa de Romeo y Julieta
iré a Santiago.
¡Oh Cuba! ¡Oh ritmo de semillas secas!
Iré a Santiago.
¡Oh cintura caliente y gota de madera!
Iré a Santiago.
¡Arpa de troncos vivos. Caimán. Flor de tabaco!
Iré a Santiago.
Siempre he dicho yo iría a Santiago
en un coche de agua negra.
Iré a Santiago.
Brisa y alcohol en las ruedas,
iré a Santiago.

SONG OF THE CUBAN BLACKS

When the full moon comes
I'll go to Santiago in Cuba.
I'll go to Santiago
in a carriage of black water.
I'll go to Santiago.
Palm-thatching will start to sing.
I'll go to Santiago.
When the palm trees want to turn into storks,
I'll go to Santiago.
When the banana trees want to turn into jellyfish,
I'll go to Santiago.
With the golden head of Fonseca.
I'll go to Santiago.
And with the rose of Romeo and Juliet
I'll go to Santiago.
Oh Cuba! Oh rhythm of dry seeds!
I'll go to Santiago.
Oh warm waist, and a drop of wood!
I'll go to Santiago.
Harp of living trees. Crocodile. Tobacco blossom!
I'll go to Santiago.
I always said I would go to Santiago
in a carriage of black water.
I'll go to Santiago.
Wind and alcohol in the wheels,
I'll go to Santiago.

Mi coral en la tiniebla,
iré a Santiago.
El mar ahogado en la arena,
iré a Santiago.
Calor blanco, fruta muerta,
iré a Santiago.
¡Oh bovino frescor de cañavera!
¡Oh Cuba! ¡Oh curva de suspiro y barro!
Iré a Santiago.

My coral in the darkness,
I'll go to Santiago.
The ocean drowned in the sand,
I'll go to Santiago.
White head and dead fruit,
I'll go to Santiago.
Oh wonderful freshness of the cane fields!
Oh Cuba! Arc of sighs and mud!
I'll go to Santiago.

from

Divan del Tamarit

1936

CASIDA DE LA ROSA

La rosa
no buscaba la aurora:
casi eterna en su ramo,
buscaba otra cosa.

La rosa,
no buscaba ni ciencia ni sombra:
confín de carne y sueño,
buscaba otra cosa.

La rosa,
no buscaba la rosa.
Inmóvil por el cielo
buscaba otra cosa.

CASIDA OF THE ROSE

The rose
was not searching for the sunrise:
almost eternal on its branch,
it was searching for something else.

The rose
was not searching for darkness or science:
borderline of flesh and dream,
it was searching for something else.

The rose
was not searching for the rose.
Motionless in the sky
it was searching for something else.

CASIDA DE LAS PALOMAS OSCURAS

A Claudio Guillén

Por las ramas del laurel
van dos palomas oscuras.
La una era el sol,
la otra la luna.
"Vecinitas," les dije,
"¿dónde está mi sepultura?"
"En mi cola," dijo el sol.
"En mi garganta," dijo la luna.
Y yo que estaba caminando
con la tierra por la cintura
vi dos águilas de nieve
y una muchacha desnuda.
La una era la otra
y la muchacha era ninguna.
"Aguilitas," les dije,
"¿dónde está mi sepultura?"
"En mi cola," dijo el sol.
"En mi garganta," dijo la luna.
Por las ramas del laurel
vi dos palomas desnudas.
La una era la otra
y las dos eran ninguna.

CASIDA OF THE SHADOWY PIGEONS

To Claudio Guillén

I saw two shadowy pigeons
in the boughs of the bay-tree.
The first was the sun,
the second was the moon.
"Hey there, little sisters," I said,
"where will I be buried?"
"Inside my tail," the sun said.
"Inside my throat," the moon said.
And I who was strolling along
with the earth around my waist
saw two snow eagles
and one naked girl.
The first was the second
and the girl wasn't either.
"Hey, little eagles," I said,
"where will I be buried?"
"Inside my tail," the sun said.
"Inside my throat," the moon said.
I saw two naked pigeons
in the branches of the bay-tree.
The first was the second
and both were neither.

CASIDA DEL LLANTO

He cerrado mi balcón
porque no quiero oír el llanto,
pero por detrás de los grises muros
no se oye otra cosa que el llanto.

Hay muy pocos ángeles que canten,
hay muy pocos perros que ladren,
mil violines caben en la palma de mi mano.

Pero el llanto es un perro inmenso,
el llanto es un ángel inmenso,
el llanto es un violín inmenso,
las lágrimas amordazan al viento,
y no se oye otra cosa que el llanto.

CASIDA OF SOBBING

I have shut my balcony door
because I don't want to hear the sobbing,
but from behind the grayish walls
nothing else comes out but sobbing.

Very few angels are singing,
very few dogs are barking,
a thousand violins fit into the palm of my hand.

But the sobbing is a gigantic dog,
the sobbing is a gigantic angel,
the sobbing is a gigantic violin,
tears close the wind's jaws,
all there is to hear is sobbing.

GACELA DE LA TERRIBLE PRESENCIA

Yo quiero que el agua se quede sin cauce.
Yo quiero que el viento se quede sin valles.

Quiero que la noche se quede sin ojos
y mi corazón sin la flor del oro;

que los bueyes hablen con las grandes hojas
y que la lombriz se muera de sombra;

que brillen los dientes de la calavera
y los amarillos inunden la seda.

Puedo ver el duelo de la noche herida
luchando enroscada con el mediodía.

Resisto un ocaso de verde veneno
y los arcos rotos donde sufre el tiempo.

Pero no ilumines tu limpio desnudo
como un negro cactus abierto en los juncos.

Déjame en un ansia de oscuros planetas,
pero no me enseñes tu cintura fresca.

GHAZAL OF THE TERRIFYING PRESENCE

I want the water to go on without its bed.
And the wind to go on without its mountain passes.

I want the night to go on without its eyes
and my heart without its golden petals;

if the oxen could only talk with the big leaves
and the angleworm would die from too much darkness;

I want the teeth in the skull to shine
and the yellowish tints to drown the silk.

I can see the night in its duel, wounded
and wrestling, tangled with noon.

I fight against a sunset of green poison,
and those broken arches where time is suffering.

But don't let the light fall on your clear and naked body
like a cactus black and open in the reeds.

Leave me in the anguish of the darkened planets,
but do not let me see your pure waist.

GACELA DE LA MUERTE OSCURA

Quiero dormir el sueño de las manzanas,
alejarme del tumulto de los cementerios.
Quiero dormir el sueño de aquel niño
que quería cortarse el corazón en alta mar.

No quiero que me repitan que los muertos no pierden la sangre;
que la boca podrida sigue pidiendo agua.
No quiero enterarme de los martirios que da la hierba,
ni de la luna con boca de serpiente
que trabaja antes del amanecer.

Quiero dormir un rato,
un rato, un minuto, un siglo;
pero que todos sepan que no he muerto;
que hay un establo de oro en mis labios;
que soy el pequeño amigo del viento Oeste;
que soy la sombra inmensa de mis lágrimas.

Cúbreme por la aurora con un velo,
porque me arrojará puñados de hormigas,
y moja con agua dura mis zapatos
para que resbale la pinza de su alacrán.

Porque quiero dormir el sueño de las manzanas
para aprender un llanto que me limpie de tierra;
porque quiero vivir con aquel niño oscuro
que quería cortarse el corazón en alta mar.

GHAZAL OF THE DARK DEATH

I want to sleep the sleep of the apples,
I want to get far away from the busyness of the cemeteries.
I want to sleep the sleep of that child
who longed to cut his heart open far out at sea.

I don't want them to tell me again how the corpse keeps all
its blood,
how the decaying mouth goes on begging for water.
I'd rather not hear about the torture sessions the grass arranges
for
nor about how the moon does all its work before dawn
with its snakelike nose.

I want to sleep for half a second,
a second, a minute, a century,
but I want everyone to know that I am still alive,
that I have a golden manger inside my lips,
that I am the little friend of the west wind,
that I am the elephantine shadow of my own tears.

When it's dawn just throw some sort of cloth over me
because I know dawn will toss fistfuls of ants at me,
and pour a little hard water over my shoes
so that the scorpion claws of the dawn will slip off.

Because I want to sleep the sleep of the apples,
and learn a mournful song that will clean all earth away from me,
because I want to live with that shadowy child
who longed to cut his heart open far out at sea.